EASY HEART - HEALTHY COOKBOOK FOR BEGINNERS

A Guide with Simple Recipes Low in Bad Fats and Salt

Wilhelmine P. Blake

TABLE OF CONTENTS

INTRODUCTION

One of the most crucial elements of overall wellness is maintaining a healthy heart. A healthy heart depends on a balanced diet, and making the appropriate food choices can help prevent cardiovascular problems. Nevertheless, selecting heart-healthy meals can be difficult, particularly for newcomers who are not familiar with the idea of a heart-healthy diet.

Filled with delicious recipes that are low in sodium, added sugar, saturated fat, and trans fat that can harm cardiovascular health, this cookbook seeks to help you select healthier foods for your meals.

With the help of the Hearth Healthy Cookbook for Beginners 2023, you can learn how to produce quick, tasty, and nutrient-dense meals. A range of options for breakfast, lunch, dinner, and even snacks are provided by the recipes. This cookbook will enable you to prepare delectable dishes that promote a healthy heart, whether you are a novice or an expert cook.

More than just a selection of recipes can be found in The Hearth Healthy Cookbook for Beginners 2023. It also offers advice on how to read food labels, the advantages of a heart-healthy diet, and how to choose healthier options when dining out. With the help of this thorough manual, you will acquire the knowledge and abilities necessary to decide on your diet intelligently, leading to a healthy lifestyle and heart.

Anyone who wishes to emphasize their heart health while still partaking in great meals should have The Hearth Healthy Cookbook for Beginners 2023 on hand. It is a great tool for people who wish to learn how to prepare healthy meals and make educated dietary decisions. You can take charge of your heart health and begin living a happier, healthier life by following the recipes and advice offered in this cookbook.

A good resource for teaching people healthy eating practices that can lower their risk of heart disease is The Hearth Healthy Cookbook for Beginners 2023. The book includes a wide range of delectable dishes that are specifically created to be low in sodium, added sugars, and saturated and trans fats, all of which are recognized risk factors for heart disease.

Knowing what to make and how to prepare it is one of the major obstacles people encounter when attempting to eat healthily. This issue is addressed by The Hearth Healthy Cookbook for Beginners 2023, which offers simple-to-follow recipes ideal for people who are new to healthy eating. The recipes employ straightforward, accessible materials and give step-by-step directions on how to make each dish.

In addition to the recipes, the book offers helpful advice on the advantages of a heart-healthy diet and how to choose healthier options when eating out. This knowledge is particularly crucial for people who are just beginning to learn about healthy eating and may not yet fully comprehend what makes up a heart-healthy diet.

Through the Hearth Healthy Cookbook for Beginners 2023, individuals can actively lower their risk of heart disease by learning healthy eating habits. The book's recipes offer a delectable and practical approach to improving one's diet without giving up taste or flavor.

The Hearth Healthy Cookbook for Beginners 2023 is a great resource for teaching people about heart-healthy eating practices. The book is certain to be a useful tool for anyone wishing to take control of their heart health and begin living a better, happier life thanks to its simple-to-follow recipes and useful information.

HEALTHY INGREDIENTS FOR HEART HEALTH

The components are necessary for a diet that is heart-healthy and the qualities they possess.

Whole grains

A diet for heart health cannot ignore the presence of whole grains, which, being unrefined, maintain their nutritional properties. The whole grain is made up of three parts: bran, the outermost part, germ, and finally, the internal part, endosperm. Rich in fiber, vitamins, minerals, and antioxidants, all essential elements for maintaining heart health.

Regular consumption of whole grains, thanks to their high fiber content, reduces the levels of LDL cholesterol (called "bad cholesterol") responsible for the development of heart disease, as well as promoting good digestion.

They contain Magnesium, Iron, Zinc and Vitamin B. These vitamins and minerals are crucial for maintaining heart health because they control blood pressure, lessen inflammation, and promote normal blood vessel activity. Whole grains contain antioxidants, including phenolic acids and flavonoids that can help lower oxidative stress and inflammation, both of which are connected to heart disease.

Some typical foods made from whole grains are quinoa, brown rice, oats, barley, bread, and pasta. These grains are adaptable and may be used in a wide range of meals, from substantial salads and grain bowls to breakfast porridges. It's critical to choose whole grains that have undergone little processing and have little to no added sugars or harmful fats.

Lean protein

Niacin, vitamin B6, iron, and other nutrients required for heart health are all found in abundance in lean protein, which includes chicken, fish, turkey, and beans. Proteins play an essential role in a heart-healthy diet because they increase the sense of satiety and maintain muscle mass. However, it is better to reduce or eliminate processed meats, which scientific evidence has been linked to an increased risk of contracting heart disease, and pick lean protein sources with a low content of saturated fat.

Healthy fats

A heart-healthy diet must include good fats, which may be found in foods like nuts, seeds, avocados, and fatty seafood like salmon and tuna. Omega-3s may lower blood pressure, reduce inflammation and cut the risk of heart illness. It's essential to choose good fats instead of dangerous saturated and trans fats. These can raise LDL cholesterol levels and increase the risk of heart disease.

Fruit

Fruits are a fantastic source of vitamins, minerals, and fiber, all of which are crucial for heart health. Antioxidants are particularly abundant in fruits like berries, citrus, and apples and can help lower inflammation and oxidative stress, both of which are associated with heart disease. Consuming a variety of fruits can assist in giving your body the nutrients it requires to keep your heart healthy. Vegetables

The vitamins, minerals, and fiber found in vegetables are vital for preserving heart health. The vitamin K found in leafy greens like spinach, kale, and Swiss chard is especially beneficial for preventing blood clotting and maintaining healthy blood vessels. Broccoli, cauliflower, and Brussels sprouts are examples of cruciferous vegetables that are high in fiber and antioxidants that can help reduce inflammation and shield against heart disease. Your diet can benefit from adding a variety of bright vegetables since they provide fiber and important nutrients for heart health.

Healthy sources of protein (legumes, nuts, fish, and seafood)

Legumes, nuts, fish, and shellfish are all nutritious sources of protein that can supply vital elements for heart health. Legumes' high protein and fiber content, such as beans, lentils, and chickpeas, reduce cholesterol levels and heart complications. Almonds, walnuts, and chia seeds are just a few examples of nuts and seeds that are high in fiber, protein, and heart-healthy fats useful for managing inflammation and reducing the risk of heart problems. Including Omega-3s in your diet can give you important nutrients and support heart health.

Liquid non-tropical vegetable oils

Canola, olive and avocado oil are non-tropical vegetable oils that are healthier alternatives to saturated and trans fats, may have an effect on LDL cholesterol levels. Due to the high concentration of mono and polyunsaturated fatty acids the LDL cholesterol levels can be lowered and the risk of heart problems reduced. These oils can contribute to the supply of vital healthy fats for heart health when used in cooking or as a salad dressing.

INGREDIENTS TO AVOID

The components and foods that are prohibited from a diet that promotes heart health

Maintaining a heart-healthy diet entails restricting or eliminating specific substances and meals that can raise the risk of heart disease, in addition to including foods that are nutrientdense. In this section, we will go through some of the substances and foods to stay away from for a heart-healthy diet.

Salt

Sodium chloride, also known as salt, is a common spice in many dishes. But too much salt can lead to high blood pressure, a major risk factor for heart illness.. For best heart health, the American Heart Association advises taking no more than 2,300 milligrams of salt per day, and ideally no more than 1,500 mg. Unfortunately, the daily salt intake of the average American is over 3,400 milligrams, which is much higher than the advised level.

The sodium content of many processed meals is significant, including frozen dinners, canned soups, and snack items. It's critical to read food labels and, whenever possible, select lowsodium products. Using fresh herbs and spices in place of salt while cooking at home can also help lower sodium intake. In addition, restricting or avoiding high-sodium condiments such as salad dressings, teriyaki sauce, and soy sauce might help lower sodium intake.

Bread and baked goods

The amount of refined carbohydrates in bread and other baked goods is frequently excessive, which can lead to weight gain and raise the risk of cardiovascular problems. Additionally, a lot of commercially produced bread and baked goods include unhealthy fats, which may raise cholesterol levels and increase the risk of cardiovascular problems.

The consumption of fiber can be increased, and heart health can be supported by choosing whole-grain bread and baked items over refined grains. Additionally, it's critical to read food labels and select goods that are low in bad fats and added sugars. As an alternative, you may help ensure you're consuming a heart-healthy product by baking homemade bread and baked items with better components like whole grain flour, canola oil, and natural sweeteners like honey or maple syrup.

Foods preserved in salt or in oil

Pickles, olives, smoked or cured meats, and other foods preserved in salt or oil are frequently high in sodium and harmful fats, which raise the risk of heart disease. In addition, a lot of these foods contain additives and preservatives that may be hazardous to your health.

It's crucial to study food labels and pick foods with little sodium and bad fats. Alternatively, cooking your own fruits and veggies, fresh or frozen, will help ensure you're getting healthy food. If you like pickled or cured foods, choosing low-sodium varieties and staying away from ones with a lot of bad fats will help lower your chance of developing heart disease.

Precooked foods

Foods that have already been cooked, such as frozen dinners, canned meals, and processed meats, are frequently high in sodium, bad fats, and chemicals. Additionally, these foods often lack fiber, vitamins, and minerals.

A wonderful way to ensure you eat a nutritious meal is to prepare it at home with fresh ingredients. It's critical to read food labels and select items that are low in sodium and bad fats when buying precooked items. Additionally, purchasing goods that are manufactured with pure, natural materials and little processing will help lower the chance of developing heart disease.

Sauces (for example mayonnaise)

Many sauces contain unhealthy fats and added sugars that can raise cholesterol levels and increase the risk of heart diseases, such as mayonnaise, ranch dressing, and barbecue sauce. In addition, a lot of sauces are heavy in salt, which might increase blood pressure.

Hummus, salsa, or homemade vinaigrette dressing are some healthier sauce options that can help lower sodium and bad fat intake. Additionally, substituting low-calorie sauces for fresh herbs and spices when flavoring food will help support heart health.

Sugary drinks and spirits

Drinks with a lot of added sugar, such as soda, sports drinks, and energy drinks, raise the risk of obesity, diabetes, and heart disease. Additionally, alcoholic drinks like beer, wine, and cocktails may contain a lot of calories, increasing the risk of weight gain and heart disease.

Instead of sugary drinks, choosing water, unsweetened tea, or low-calorie beverages can help lower sugar intake and support heart health. The probability of heart complications can also be decreased by keeping alcohol consumption to moderate levels. My advice would be to eliminate it altogether, because alcohol content is always harmful, especially in the long term.

In addition to including heart-healthy items in your diet, you should also limit or avoid some substances that raise your chance of developing heart disease. Foods preserved in salt or oil, bread, and baked products heavy in refined carbs and harmful fats and high in sodium should all be avoided or limited in order to support heart health. It's critical to read food labels and, whenever possible, pick items that are low in sodium and bad fats. You may also help ensure that you're consuming a heart-healthy product by making homemade versions of bread and baked items with healthier ingredients. You can lessen your chance of developing heart disease and improve your general health and well-being by making simple dietary changes and restricting or eliminating dangerous foods and substances.

BREAKFAST RECIPES

A heart-healthy diet does not have to be uninteresting or bland. With the recipes in this cookbook, you can prepare heart-healthy meals that are delectable and nutritious. Choose foods that have been minimally processed and limit your consumption of saturated and trans fats, sodium, and added carbohydrates. joyful hearts and joyful kitchens!

Egg Muffins with Spinach and Mushrooms

These Egg Muffins with Spinach and Mushrooms are an ideal grab-and-go brunch option. Protein-, vitamin-, and mineral-rich, they are not only tasty but also nutritious. With their combination of spinach, mushrooms, and eggs, these pastries make for a hearty morning meal.

Ingredients:

- 6 large eggs
- 1 cup finely sliced spinach
- ½ cup mushroom slices
- ¼ cup chopped scallions
- ¼ cup of grated low-fat cheese (such as mozzarella or cheddar).
- ¼ teaspoon salt
- ¼ milligram black pepper

Preparation Guidelines:

1. Heat the oven to 175C/350F and grease a muffin tin with olive oil.
2. Pour some olive oil into the frying pan over medium-high heat. Add the diced onions and mushroom slices and cook until softened approximately 5 minutes.
3. In a mixing basin, thoroughly combine the eggs. Add the minced spinach, mushrooms, onions, cheese, salt, and black pepper. Stir to incorporate.
4. Spoon the egg mixture evenly into the muffin tray, filling each cup to approximately three-quarters capacity.
5. Bake the egg muffins in a preheated oven for about 20 or until set and faintly golden on top.
6. Remove from the oven. Leave to set for a few minutes. Using a knife, loosen the muffins' edges and place them on a cooling tray to cool completely.
7. Once chilled, these egg muffins can be refrigerated for up to 4 days. You can consume them chilled or reheat them in the microwave for a speedy breakfast.

Nutrition analysis per serving (1 egg muffin):

- Calories 80
- Fats 5g (1.5g Sat fat; 0g Trans Fat)
- Sodium 130mg
- Carbs 2g Fibers 0.5g
- Sugars 1g
- Proteins 7g

Shopping List:

- Eggs
- Spinach
- Mushrooms
- Onion
- Garlic
- Salt
- Black pepper

Whole Wheat Pancakes with Fresh Berries

These Whole Wheat Pancakes with Fresh Berries are a delicious and nutritious way to begin the day. Made with whole wheat flour and garnished with a rainbow of fresh berries, they provide a breakfast that is rich in fiber and antioxidants. These pancakes are light and flavorful, making them an ideal breakfast delight.

Ingredients:

- 1 cup 100 % whole wheat flour
- 1 tsp sugar
- 1 tsp baking powder
- ½ tsp baking soda
- ¼ tsp salt
- 1 pint of buttermilk
- 1 large egg
- 1 tbsp melted unsalted butter (or vegetable oil)
- 1 tsp vanilla extract
- Topping with fresh berries (such as blueberries, strawberries, or raspberries).
- Maple syrup for serve

Preparation Guidelines:

1. Mix the wholemeal flour, baking powder, sugar, salt, and baking soda in a large bowl.
2. Whisk together the buttermilk, egg, oil or butter, and vanilla extract in an another receptacle until thoroughly mixed.
3. Fold the liquid ingredients into the dry ingredients and mix gently. Do not overmix; chunks are acceptable.
4. Heat a coated frying pan over a medium heat and lightly grease with cooking oil or butter
5. Pour ¼ cup pancake batter into the pan. Turn and fry until golden brown.
6. Serve warm crêpes with plenty of fresh berries and drizzle with maple syrup.

Nutrition analysis per serving (2 crepes with berries and syrup):

- Calories 250
- Fats 6g (3g of sat fat - 0g Trans Fat)
- Cholesterol 60 mg
- Sodium 400mg
- Carbs: 42g
- Fibers 5g
- Sugars 9g
- Proteins 8g

Shopping List:

- Egg
- Whole wheat flour
- Baking powder
- Baking soda
- Milk
- Salt
- Vanilla extract
- Berries (strawberries, blueberries, raspberries, etc.)

Greek Yogurt Parfait with Granola and Fruits

This Greek Yogurt Parfait with Granola and Fruit is a delectable and healthy breakfast option that combines the creaminess of Greek yogurt with the crunchiness of granola and the sweetness of fresh fruit. It is a nutritious and satisfying meal that provides protein, fiber, and vitamins to fuel your day.

Ingredients:

- 1 cup unsweetened Greek yogurt
- Optional: 1 teaspoonful of honey or maple syrup
- For the ½ cup serving, choose a wholegrain, low-sugar cereal.
- ½ cup of fresh mixed fruit, including blueberries, strawberries, and raspberries.
- Optional: ¼ cup sliced almonds or minced walnuts

Preparation Guidelines:

1. To add sweetness, combine Greek yogurt with honey or maple syrup in a small basin.
2. Layer mid of the Greek yogurt in a serving glass or basin.
3. Mdof the granola should be sprinkled over the yogurt layer.
4. Add one-half of the fresh mixed berries to the granola.
5. Layer the remaining Greek yogurt, granola, and fresh berries.
6. Almonds or walnuts can be sprinkled on the top layer for added texture and flavor.
7. Serve the Greek Yogurt Parfait immediately or chill for up to one hour to enable the flavors to meld.
8. Enjoy this wholesome and refreshing breakfast delight!

Nutritional analysis per serving:

- Calories 350
- Fats 12g (2g of sat - 0g Trans)
- Cholesterol 5mg
- Sodium 90mg
- Carbs 46g
- Fibers 6g
- Sugars 19g
- Proteins 20g

Shopping List:

- Greek yogurt
- Granola
- Honey
- Fruit (such as berries, bananas, or apples)

Oatmeal with Chia Seeds and Almonds

This Oatmeal with Chia Seeds and Almonds is a nourishing and soothing breakfast that will keep you energized for the duration of the morning. Oats are a great source of fiber, while chia seeds add omega-3. This breakfast delicacy is the perfect combination of flavors and textures, topped with crunchy almonds.

Ingredients:

- ½ ounce of rolled oats
- 1 cup unadulterated almond milk (or your preferred milk)
- 1.25 grams chia seeds
- ¼ tsp vanilla extract
- 1 teaspoon maple syrup or honey (optional sweetener)
- 2 tbsp of almonds, cut
- Fresh cherries as a garnish

Preparation Guidelines:

1. Mix the almond milk, oats, chia seeds, maple syrup or honey (if using), and vanilla extract in a pan.
2. Boil over medium heat, stirring occasionally.
3. Lower the heat and simmer for 5 to 7 minutes or until oats are soft and mixture is thick. Periodically stir to prevent adhering.
4. Allow the oatmeal to rest for one minute before removing from the heat.
5. Add sliced almonds and fresh berries to the top of the oatmeal in the serving basin.
6. Enjoy this wholesome and satisfying breakfast served steaming.

Nutritional analysis per serving:

- Calories 300
- Fats 12g (1 g Sat - 0g Trans)
- Cholesterol 0mg
- Sodium 80mg
- Carbs 38g
- Fibers 8g Sugars 9g
- Proteins 9g

Shopping List:

- Oats
- Milk
- Water
- Chia seeds
- Almonds
- Honey or maple syrup(optional)

Avocado Toast with Poached Egg

This Avocado Toast with Poached Egg is a simple and wholesome breakfast that is loaded with healthful fats, protein, and fiber. The avocado spread on whole grain toast is topped with a perfectly poached egg to create a delectable and filling breakfast.

Ingredients:

- 2 slices 100% whole wheat bread
- 1 mature avocado
- juice of half a lemon
- pepper and salt to flavor
- 2 large embryos
- 1 teaspoon of white vinegar (to be used for poaching).
- Red pepper flakes and minced fresh herbs (such as cilantro or chives) are optional garnishes.

Preparation Guidelines:

1. Toast the slices of whole grain bread until they reach the desired crispiness.
2. While the bread is being toasted, halve the ripe avocado, remove the seed, and put meat in a bowl. Add lemon juice, salt, and pepper. Mash the avocado until it reaches the desirable consistency.
3. In a separate saucepan place water. Combine the white vinegar and water.
4. One egg should be cracked into a tiny bowl or ramekin. Using a spoon, create a gentle whirlpool in the simmering water, then insert the egg into the center of the whirlpool. Repeat with another egg.
5. The eggs should be poached for approximately 3 to 4 minutes. Remove them from the water and place on a paper towel-lined plate .
6. Spread the avocado on the toasted bread slices evenly.
7. Place an egg poached on each avocado crostini.
8. If desired, add more salt, pepper, red pepper flakes, and minced fresh herbs.
9. Serve immediately and savor this nourishing and delectable breakfast.

Analysis of nutrition per serving (2 avocado toasts with poached eggs):

- Calories 400
- Fats 22g (4g Sat Fat - 0g Trans)
- Sodium: 400mg
- Carbs 35g
- Fibers 12g
- Sugars 3g
- Proteins 20g

Shopping List:

- Whole grain bread
- Avocado
- Egg
- Salt
- Black pepper
- Lemon juice

Veggie Breakfast Burritos

These Veggie Breakfast Burritos are a delicious and filling way to start the day. These burritos are a complete supper on their own due to the presence of colorful vegetables and proteinrich black beans. Wrap them in whole wheat tortillas for a portable, nutritious breakfast option.

Ingredients:

- Four flour tortillas
- 1 teaspoonful olive oil
- ½ scarlet bell pepper, diced
- ½ small minced red onion
- ½ green bell pepper, sliced
- 1 cup strained and rinsed black beans
- 1 teaspoon cumin powder
- ½ milligram of chili spice
- pepper and salt to flavor
- 4 whisked eggs
- ¼ cup of reduced-fat cheddar cheese shreds
- Condiments include salsa, avocado segments, and Greek yogurt (optional)

Preparation Guidelines:

1. In a large frying pan, heat olive oil over medium heat. Add the diced red onion and bell peppers. They are cooked for approximately 5 minutes or until they have softened.
2. Combine the black beans, powdered cumin, chili powder, salt, and pepper in a skillet. Stir to combine and cook for 2 to 3 minutes or until the beans are thoroughly heated.
3. Place the beaten eggs on the opposite side of the skillet from the vegetables and legumes. Scramble the eggs until they reach the desired consistency.
4. In a skillet, combine the scrambled eggs with the vegetable and legume mixture. Stir to incorporate.
5. The whole wheat tortillas should be heated in a separate skillet or microwave.
6. Evenly distribute the egg and vegetable mixture between the tortillas. Top each portion with shredded cheddar cheese.
7. Add garnishes of choice, such as salsa, avocado slices, or Greek yogurt.
8. As you roll the tortillas into burritos, fold the sides.
9. Warm the Veggie fare Burritos and savor this flavorful and wholesome fare.

Nutritional analysis per serving:

- Calories 320
- Fats 10g (2g of Sat – 0g Trans)
- Sodium 480mg
- Carbs 42g
- Fibers 9g
- Sugars 4g
- Proteins 17g

Shopping List:

- Whole wheat tortillas
- Eggs
- Bell peppers
- Onion
- Garlic
- Spinach
- Salt
- Black pepper
- Cheese (optional)

Quinoa Breakfast Bowl with Mixed Berries

This Quinoa Breakfast Bowl with Mixed Berries is a nutritious and delicious way to begin the day. Quinoa is a complete protein, and when combined with fresh berries, it makes for a scrumptious and filling breakfast. Customize this bowl with your preferred garnishes to create a delicious breakfast treat.

Ingredients:

- ¼ cup prepared quinoa
- 0.5 ounces of assorted berries (including strawberries, blueberries, and raspberries).
- 1 gram of honey or maple syrup
- 2 tablespoons of minced nuts (like almonds, walnuts, or pecans)
- Optional garnishes include Greek yogurt, chia seeds, shredded coconut, and almond butter drizzle.

Preparation Guidelines:

1. Cook quinoa according to package directions, then allow it to settle.
2. Mix the cooked quinoa and assorted berries in a serving bowl.
3. Honey or maple syrup may be drizzled over the quinoa and fruit.
4. To add texture and flavor, sprinkle the top with chopped pecans.
5. Add desired garnishes, such as a dollop of Greek yogurt, chia seeds, shredded coconut, or almond butter drizzle.
6. Combine the ingredients by gently mixing them.
7. Serve the Quinoa Breakfast Bowl immediately and savor this nutritious and delectable breakfast.

Nutritional analysis per serving:

- Calories 280
- Fats 10g (1g Sat - 0g Trans)
- Cholesterol 0mg
- Sodium 5mg
- Carbs 42g
- Fibers 6g
- Sugars 12g
- Proteins 8g

Shopping List:

- Quinoa
- Milk
- Water
- Mixed berries (strawberries, blueberries, raspberries, etc.)
- Honey or maple syrup (optional)

-

Blueberry Almond Smoothie Bowl

This Blueberry Almond Smoothie Bowl is an energizing and nutrient-rich breakfast option that incorporates blueberries, almonds, and Greek yogurt. This smoothie bowl, topped with granola and additional berries, is a burst of flavor and texture.

Ingredients:

- ½ banana
- 1 cup frozen blackberries
- ½ cup unsweetened Greek yogurt
- ½ cup sugar-free almond milk
- 1g of almond butter
- Fresh blueberries, sliced almonds, granola, chia seeds, and honey are optional garnishes.
- Almond butter
- Honey or maple syrup (optional)

Preparation Guidelines:

1. Blend the thawed blueberries, ripe bananas, almond milk, Greek yogurt, and almond butter together.
2. Mix until smooth and velvety; if necessary, add almond milk to achieve the desired consistency.
3. The smoothie is poured into a dish.
4. Honey is drizzled over blueberries, almonds, granola, chia seeds, and granola.
5. Serve the Blueberry Almond Smoothie Bowl immediately, and enjoy this scrumptious and wholesome breakfast.

Nutritional analysis per serving:

- Calories 320
- Fats: 11g (1g Sat – 0g Trans)
- Cholesterol 5mg
- Sodium: 120mg
- Carbs 44g
- Fibers 9g
- Sugars 24g
- Proteins 17g

Shopping List:

- Frozen blueberries
- Almond milk
- Greek yogurt

Sweet Potato Hash with Turkey Sausage

This Sweet Potato Hash with Turkey Sausage is a substantial, flavorful, and nutrient-dense breakfast choice. The combination of sweet potatoes, lean turkey sausage, and colorful vegetables creates a delectable and filling breakfast that will keep you energized all morning.

Ingredients:

- 2 medium sweet potatoes, trimmed and diced
- 8 ounces casing-free turkey sausage, lean
- ½ green bell pepper, sliced
- ½ small minced red onion
- 2 chopped garlic cloves
- ½ scarlet bell pepper, diced
- 1 teaspoon rosemary leaves
- pepper and salt to flavor
- 2 teaspoons olive oil
- Optional garnishes include minced fresh parsley and hot sauce

Preparation Guidelines:

1. Over medium heat, put a drizzle of olive oil into a large skillet.
2. Add potato cubes and cook until golden brown and soft (about 10 min.)
3. In a separate frying pan, brown the turkey sausage and continue to fry over medium heat until it is cooked through. Break the sausage into small crumbles.
4. Take the cooked sweet potatoes from the frying pan and set them to one side.
5. Add the diced peppers, red onion, chopped garlic, dried thyme, salt, and pepper in the same frying pan. Cook the vegetables for about 5 minutes or until soft.
6. Add the sweet potatoes and turkey sausage to the sautéed vegetables in the skillet. Stir to incorporate.
7. Cook for another 2-3 minutes or until all flavors are combined, and the dish is thoroughly heated.
8. If desirable, garnish the Sweet Potato Hash with chopped fresh parsley after removing it from the heat.
9. If you enjoy a touch of spice, serve the hash with a dash of hot sauce.

Nutritional analysis per serving:

- Calories 320
- Fats 12g (2g Sat – 0g Trans)
- Cholesterol 40 mg
- Sodium 480mg
- Carbs 38g
- Fibers 6g
- Sugars 10g
- Proteins 18g

Shopping List:

- Sweet potato
- Onion
- Garlic
- Turkey sausage
- Bell pepper
- Salt
- Black pepper
- Olive oil

MAIN DISHES RECIPES

Grilled Lemon and Herb Chicken with Quinoa Salad

This Grilled Lemon Herb Chicken with Quinoa Salad is an ideal primary dish for a healthy lunch or dinner because it is light and flavorful. The grilled chicken is marinated in a zesty lemon herb sauce, and it combines beautifully with the vegetable- and herb-filled quinoa salad.

Ingredients:

For the Lemon Herb Grilled Chicken:

- Four skinless and boneless chicken breasts
- Lemon zest and juice of 1
- 2 teaspoons olive oil
- 2 minced garlic cloves
- 1 tsp powdered dry Oregano
- 1 tsp rosemary leaves
- pepper and salt to flavor

For the Quinoa Salad, combine:

- 1 cucumber, sliced
- 1 cup prepared quinoa
- ½ red scallion, minced finely
- 1 cup halved cherry tomatoes
- ¼ cup minced parsley
- ¼ cup freshly cut mint
- Lemon juice
- 2 tbsp extra-virgin olive oil
- pepper and salt to flavor

Preparation Guidelines:

For the Lemon Herb Grilled Chicken:

1. Mix the olive oil, lemon zest, lemon juice, minced garlic, dry oregano, dry thyme, salt, and pepper in a basin.
2. Place the chicken breasts in a shallow bowl and pour the marinade on top. Ensure that the chicken is evenly coated.
3. Cover the dish and marinate the chicken in the refrigerator for about 30 minutes, or up to one day, for optimal flavor.
4. The grill should be heated to medium heat.
5. Take the chicken out of the marinade.
6. Cook 6/8 minutes per side.
7. Once cooked, take off the grill and let rest for a few minutes before cutting.
8. *For the Quinoa Salad, combine:*
9. In a large bowl, mix together the cooked quinoa, the cherry tomatoes, the diced cucumber, the chopped red onion, the chopped parsley and the chopped mint.
10. Whisk lemon juice, olive oil, salt and pepper in a small bowl.
11. Drizzle the dressing over the quinoa salad and toss to combine.
12. Adapt the seasoning as necessary.

To Provide:

1. Slice the lemon herb grilled chicken.
2. On each plate, distribute the quinoa salad and cover with the chicken.
3. If preferred, garnish with additional fresh herbs.
4. Serve the Lemon Herb Grilled Chicken with Quinoa Salad and savor this delectable and wholesome main dish.

Nutritional analysis per serving:

- Calories 350
- Fats 12g (2g Sat – 0g Trans)
- Cholesterol 80mg
- Sodium 200mg
- Carbs 30g
- Fibers 5g
- Sugars 3g
- Proteins 30g

Shopping List :

- Chicken breast
- Quinoa
- Lemon
- Garlic
- Fresh herbs (such as thyme and parsley)
- Cherry tomatoes
- Cucumber
- Red onion
- Feta cheese (optional)

Salmon with roasted vegetables

This Baked Salmon with Roasted Vegetables is a nutritious and flavorful dish that highlights the natural opulence of salmon and the vibrant flavors of roasted vegetables. The salmon fillets are seasoned with seasonings and baked to perfection, while the roasted vegetables provide a colorful, nutritious side dish.

Ingredients:

- 4 salmon fillets
- 1 tsp olive oil
- 2 minced garlic cloves
- 1 tsp dry dill
- 1 tsp rosemary leaves
- pepper and salt to flavor
- 2 cups diced assorted vegetables
- 2 tsp vinegar
- 1 tsp of honey
- 1 teaspoonful mustard made with whole grain
- Fresh parsley may be used as a garnish (optional).

Preparation Guidelines:

1. Start to heat the oven to 400°F(200°C).
2. Place the salmon fillets on an aluminum foil- or parchment-lined baking sheet.
3. In a small basin, combine the olive oil, minced garlic, dried dill, dried thyme, salt, and pepper.
4. Spread the herb mixture evenly on both sides of the salmon fillets.
5. Combine the mixed vegetables with honey, mustard, and balsamic vinegar in a separate receptacle. Turn the vegetables to coat evenly.
6. Arrange the vegetables on a single baking tray.
7. Place the salmon and vegetables in an oven that has been preheated.
8. Bake for about 20 minutes, flake readily with a fork, and the vegetables are soft and caramelized.
9. Take the salmon and the vegetables out of the oven.
10. Serve the roasted vegetables alongside the broiled salmon.
11. If desirable, garnish with fresh parsley.

Nutritional analysis per serving:

- Calories 380
- Fats 18g (3g Sat – 0g Trans)
- Cholesterol 70 mg
- Sodium 250mg
- Carbs 20g
- Fibers 4g
- Sugars 12g
- Proteins 32g

Shopping List:

- Salmon fillets
- Sweet potato
- Broccoli
- Carrots
- Olive oil
- Salt and pepper
- Lemon

Vegetable and Lentil Stir-Fry

This Lentil and Vegetable Stir-Fry is a quick and healthy main dish loaded with plant-based protein and an assortment of colorful vegetables. The combination of protein-rich lentils, crisp vegetables, and flavorful stir-fry sauce creates a tasty and nutritious entrée.

Ingredients:

- 1 cup dry legumes
- 2 gallons water
- 1 Shallot, sliced
- 2 carrots, cut
- 2 teaspoons olive oil
- 1 bell pepper, cut
- 2 cups broccoli florets
- 2 minced garlic cloves
- 1-inch ginger root, sliced
- 2 tbsp of soy sauce with minimal sodium
- 1 tsp of rice vinegar
- 1 gram of honey (to taste maple syrup)
- 1 teaspoon cornflour
- ¼ cup liquid
- Pepper and salt to flavor
- Green scallions and sesame seeds may be added as a topping.

Preparation Guidelines:

1. Rinse the legumes with cold water.
2. Bring two cups of water to a boil in a medium-sized saucepan. Add the lentils and reduce the heat to low. Simmer lentils for approximately 15 to 20 minutes or until tender. Drain and set aside any excess water.
3. In a large fry pan, heat the olive oil on medium heat.
4. Add the sliced onion, carrots, bell pepper, and broccoli florets. Stir-fry the vegetables for about 5 to 7 minutes or until they are crisp-tender.
5. Add the garlic and ginger to the space created by moving the vegetables to one side of the pan. Stir-fry for about 30 seconds to infuse the oil with their seasonings.
6. Combine the soy sauce, rice vinegar, honey or maple syrup, cornstarch, and ¼ cup water in a small bowl and stir until smooth.
7. The sauce mixture should be poured over the vegetables in the skillet. To evenly coat the vegetables, stir well.
8. Add the cooked legumes to the pan and stir-fry for two to three minutes.
9. Season to flavor with salt and pepper.
10. Remove from heat and transfer to serving dishes.

Nutritional analysis per serving:

- Calories 280
- Fats 7g (1g Sat – 0g Trans)
- Cholesterol 0mg
- Sodium 350mg
- Carbs 44g
- Fibers 12g
- Sugars 9g
- Proteins 14g

Shopping List:

- Lentils
- Broccoli
- Carrots
- Bell peppers
- Onion
- Garlic
- Soy sauce
- Ginger
- Sesame oil

Turkey and Vegetable Lettuce Wraps

These lettuce wraps with turkey and vegetables are a delectable and light option for a heart-healthy main course. Turkey ground with aromatic seasonings is cooked with a variety of vegetables. The vibrant and flavorful filling is then enveloped in crisp lettuce leaves to create a scrumptious and healthy meal.

Ingredients:

- 1 onion, sliced
- 2 minced garlic cloves
- 1 pound lean turkey minced
- 1 teaspoonful olive oil
- 1 zucchini, sliced
- 1 carrot, minced
- 1 bell pepper, sliced
- 2 tbps of soy sauce with minimal sodium
- 1 teaspoon ful hoisin sauce
- 1 tsp ginger powder
- 1 tsp cumin powder
- optional ½ tsp chili powder
- pepper and salt to flavor
- Wrapping lettuce fronds (such as butter lettuce or iceberg lettuce).
- Optional garnishes include minced peanuts and fresh cilantro

Preparation Guidelines:

1. Start by heating some olive oil in a large frying pan over moderate heat.
2. Incorporate the garlic and the onion into the pan. Sauté the onion for two to three minutes or until translucent.
3. Add the turkey powder to the frying pan . Cook the turkey, breaking it up with a spatula, until it is browned and fully cooked.
4. Add minced bell pepper, zucchini, and carrot to the pan. Cooking for an additional 4 or 5 min. or until they are crisp-tender.
5. Whisk together the low-sodium soy sauce, hoisin sauce, ginger powder, cumin powder, chili flakes (if using), salt, and pepper in a small basin.
6. Pour the sauce mixture over the skillet's turkey and vegetable mixture. Stir well to evenly coat the ingredients.
7. Cooking for another 2 to 3 minutes to enable the flavors to combine.
8. Take the skillet off the heat and allow it to settle.
9. To create wrappers, spoon the turkey and vegetable filling onto the lettuce leaves.If desirable, garnish with chopped peanuts and fresh cilantro.
10. Serve the Turkey and Vegetable Lettuce Wraps as a savory and nutritious main course.

Nutritional analysis per serving:

- Calories 250
- Fats 11g (2g Sat – 0g Trans)
- Cholesterol: 60 mg
- Sodium 450mg
- Carbs 13g
- Fibers 3g
- Sugars 6g
- Proteins 25g

Shopping List:

- Ground turkey
- Lettuce leaves
- Carrots
- Bell peppers
- Cucumber
- Green onion
- Hoisin sauce
- Soy sauce
- Rice vinegar
- Garlic
- Ginger

Quinoa Stuffed Bell Peppers

These Quinoa-Stuffed Bell Peppers are a flavorful and healthy main dish combining protein-rich quinoa and various vegetables. The bell peppers function as a tasty consumable container and a vibrant addition to the filling. This dish is a nutritious and delicious option for lunch or dinner, as it is rich in vitamins, minerals, and fiber.

Ingredients:

- Four large jalapenos of any color
- 1 cup prepared quinoa
- 1 teaspoonful olive oil
- 1 onion, sliced
- 2 minced garlic cloves
- 1 carrot, sliced
- 1 zucchini, sliced
- 1 cup minced fresh or canned tomatoes
- 1 tsp powdered dried oregano
- 1 tsp dried basil
- pepper and salt to flavor
- ½cup grated mozzarella cheese (optional)
- Fresh parsley may be used as a garnish (optional).

Preparation Guidelines:

1. Start by preheating the oven to 375°F/190°C.
2. Remove the seeds and skin from the chilies by cutting off the stems. Put to one side.
3. Heat olive oil in a large skillet over a medium heat.
4. Incorporate the onion and garlic into the pan. Sauté the onion for two to three minutes or until translucent.
5. Carrot and zucchini should be added to the skillet. Cook the vegetables for about 5-6 min or until they are faintly tender.
6. Incorporate the cooked quinoa, diced tomatoes, dried oregano, dried basil, salt, and pepper into a bowl. Continue cook for another 2 to 3 minutes to enable the flavors to combine.
7. Take the pan away from the fire.
8. Pack the quinoa and vegetable mixture securely into the bell peppers that have been hollowed out.
9. Place the peppers in an erect position in a baking dish.
10. If desired, crown each stuffed bell pepper with shreds of mozzarella cheese.
11. Cover with a sheet of aluminum foil. Bake for about 25 min.
12. Remove the foil. Bake for another 10 min until the peppers are soft, and the cheese is golden.
13. Allow the stuffed bell peppers to settle for about 2 or 3 min, then remove them from the oven.
14. If desirable, garnish with fresh parsley.
15. Serve the Quinoa-Stuffed Bell Peppers as a nutritious and delectable main course.

Nutritional analysis per serving:

- Calories 240
- Fats 6g (1g Sat – 0g Trans)
- Cholesterol 0mg
- Sodium 280mg
- Carbs 40g
- Fibers 8g
- Sugars 10g
- Proteins 10g

Shopping List:

- Bell peppers
- Quinoa
- Onion
- Garlic
- Black beans
- Canned diced tomatoes
- Cumin
- Chili powder
- Cheese (optional)

Squash Spaghetti with Tomato Basil Sauce

This Spaghetti Squash with Tomato Basil Sauce is a healthier and lower-carb option to traditional pasta dishes. The spaghetti squash is roasted to perfection before being crowned with a tomato basil sauce. It is a satiating and nutrient-dense main course loaded with vitamins, minerals, and fiber.

Ingredients:

- 2 tsp olive oil
- 1 spaghetti squash
- 2 minced garlic cloves
- 1 onion, sliced
- ¼ cup tomato paste
- 14-ounce can of pureed tomatoes
- 1 tsp powdered dried oregano
- 1 tsp dry basil
- pepper and salt to flavor

Optional fresh basil stems for garnish Parmesan cheese grated for serving (optional)

Preparation Guidelines:

1. Preheat the oven to 400°F /200°C.
2. Halve the spaghetti squash along its length. Remove the seeds and dispose of them.
3. Coat the sides of the spaghetti squash cut with 1 tbsp of olive oil.
4. Place the halves, cut facing down, on a parchment-lined baking sheet.
5. The spaghetti squash should be roasted in a preheated oven for 40 to 50 min or until the flesh is tender and separates readily with a fork. Allow it to chill for several minutes.
6. While roasting the spaghetti squash, prepare the tomato basil sauce.
7. Warm the remaining oil in a large frying pan over medium heat.
8. Incorporate garlic and onion into the pan. Sauté the onion for about 2 to 3 minutes or until translucent and aromatic.
9. Combine the pureed tomatoes, tomato paste, dry basil, dry oregano, salt, and pepper in a skillet. Mix thoroughly to incorporate.
10. Allow the sauce to simmer for approximately 15 min, stirring occasionally, to allow the flavors to meld.
11. Using a utensil, separate the strands of flesh from the roasted spaghetti squash.
12. Distribute the strands of spaghetti squash among serving dishes.
13. The tomato basil sauce should be poured over the spaghetti squash.
14. If desirable, garnish with fresh basil leaves and serve with Parmesan cheese on the side.
15. Spaghetti Squash with Tomato Basil Sauce is a nutritious and flavorful main course.

Nutritional analysis per serving:

- Calories 180
- Fats 8g (1g Sat – 0g Trans)
- Cholesterol 0mg
- Sodium 290mg
- Carbs 27g
- Fibers 7g
- Sugars 14g
- Proteins 4g

Shopping List:

- Spaghetti squash
- Onion
- Garlic
- Canned crushed tomatoes
- Fresh basil
- Olive oil
- Salt and pepper
- Parmesan cheese (optional)

Brown Rice and Grilled Shrimp Skewers

These Grilled Shrimp Skewers with Brown Rice are a delectable and light central dish ideal for summertime grilling. The shrimp are skewered, marinated in an aromatic blend of seasonings, and grilled to perfection. This dish is served with fluffy brown rice and protein, and healthy cereals.

Ingredients:

- 1 pound of skinned and deveined large shrimp
- 2 tsp olive oil
- 2 minced garlic cloves
- ½ milligram of chili spice
- 1 tsp allspice
- 0.5 milligram powdered cumin
- Optional: ¼ tsp cayenne pepper for added spice.
- pepper and salt to flavor
- 2 cups brown rice
- serving segments of lemon
- Fresh parsley may be used as a garnish (optional).

Preparation Guidelines:

1. Heat the grill (or barbecue) to a medium temperature.
2. Mix the olive oil, garlic, paprika, chili, cumin, cayenne pepper (if using), salt, and pepper in a basin. Mix thoroughly to create a marinade.
3. Add shrimp that has been skinned and deveined to the marinade. Leave them to marinate for a further 15 minutes.
4. While the shrimp marinates, prepare the rice in accordance with container instructions. Set aside.
5. Ensure to leave a little space between each prawn when threading them onto skewers.
6. Place the shrimp skewers on a barbecue that has been preheated. Cook until opaque and pink in color (for 2 to 3 minutes on each side)
7. The shrimp skewers should be removed from the grill and allowed to settle for a few minutes.
8. Distribute the cooked brown rice between dishes.
9. Place the shrimp skewers that have been grilled atop the brown rice.
10. Fresh lemon juice should be squeezed over the prawns and rice.
11. If desirable, garnish with fresh parsley.
12. Serve the Grilled Shrimp Skewers with Brown Rice as a protein-rich and flavorful main course.

Nutritional analysis per serving:

- Calories 320
- Fats 9g (1g Sat – 0g Trans)
- Sodium 350mg
- Carbs 34g
- Fibers 3g
- Sugars 0g
- Proteins 26g

Shopping List:

- Shrimp
- Bell peppers
- Red onion
- Pineapple
- Brown rice
- Soy sauce
- Honey
- Garlic
- Ginger

Cod baked with a lemon-dill sauce

This Baked Cod with Lemon-Dill Sauce is a flavorful and light main dish that accentuates the delicate flavors of cod. Herb-seasoned cod fillets are baked to perfection and served with a tart and velvety lemon-dill sauce. This dish is straightforward yet elegant, ideal for a formal dinner or a quick weeknight meal.

Ingredients:

- 4 cod fillets (each approximately 6 ounces)
- ½ milligram of garlic flour
- 1 tsp dried dill
- 2 tsp olive oil
- 1 teaspoonful lemon juice
- 1 tsp lemon juice
- 1 tsp fresh minced dill
- pepper and salt to flavor
- Lemon-Dill Sauce
- 1 ounce of Greek yogurt
- pepper and salt

Preparation Guidelines:

1. Preheat the oven to 400°F/200°C.
2. Place cod fillets in a baking tray. They should be drizzled with oil and lemon juice.
3. Combine the dried dill, garlic powder, pepper, and salt in a small basin.
4. The herb mixture should be equally distributed over the cod fillets.
5. Bake the cod until it flakes readily and is thoroughly cooked (for 12 to 15 min).
6. Prepare the lemon-dill sauce while the cod is cooking. Thoroughly mix the Greek yogurt, lemon juice, fresh dill, salt, and pepper in a basin with a whisk.
7. After the cod has finished roasting, take it out and leave it to cool down for a minute or two.
8. On top of the broiled cod fillets, place a dollop of lemon-dill sauce.
9. If preferred, garnish with additional fresh dill.
10. Enjoy the Baked Cod with Lemon-Dill Sauce as a flavorful and light main course.

Nutritional analysis per serving:

- Calories 220
- Fats 8g (1g Sat – 0g Trans)
- Cholesterol: 65 mg
- Sodium 120mg
- Carbs 4g
- Fibers 0g
- Sugars 2g
- Proteins 32g

Shopping List:

- Cod fillets
- Lemon
- Dill
- Greek yogurt
- Garlic
- Olive oil
- Salt and pepper

Chickpea and Vegetable Curry

This Chickpea and Vegetable Curry is a flavorful and hearty main dish that combines the rich flavors of Indian seasonings with an assortment of vegetables. The flavorful curry sauce and velvety chickpeas make for a satiating and nutritious entrée. Serve it alongside steamed rice or heated naan bread for a complete and delectable meal.

Ingredients:

- 2 tsp vegetable oil
- 2 minced garlic cloves
- 1 onion, sliced
- 1 tsp cumin powder
- 1 tsp minced ginger
- 1 tsp curcuma
- 1 tsp of coriander powder
- ½ teaspoon paprika
- ¼ tsp cayenne pepper (modify flavor as desired).
- 1 can of pureed tomatoes
- 1 can of coconut milk
- 2 cups diced assorted vegetables (including bell peppers, carrots, peas, and potatoes)
- 1 can of drained and rinsed legumes
- Salt to flavor
- Fresh cilantro is an optional garnish.
- Serve with steamed rice or naan bread.

Preparation Guidelines:

1. Heat the vegetable oil over medium heat.
2. Fry the diced onion in a pan until translucent and golden.
3. Stir in garlic and ginger and simmer for another minute. Combine the ground cumin, powdered coriander, turmeric, paprika, and cayenne pepper in a skillet. Stir thoroughly to coat the onions and seasonings evenly.
4. Add the tomato cubes and liquid and cook until starting to break down (for a few minutes)
5. Once you have incorporated the coconut milk, bring the mixture to the boil.
6. In a skillet, combine the diced vegetables and legumes. Stir to integrate all ingredients.
7. Lower heat, cover the pan, and cook curry until vegetables are tender and tastes are blended (15 to 20 minutes).
8. The curry should be tasted and salted as required.
9. Take the frying pan off the heat. Leave the sauce to thicken for a few minutes.
10. Serve the Chickpea and Vegetable Curry with heated naan bread or steamed rice.
11. If desirable, garnish with fresh cilantro.
12. As a satisfying main entrée, try the flavorful and comforting Chickpea and Vegetable Curry.

Nutritional analysis per serving:

- Calories 320
- Fats20g (12g Sat – 0g Trans)
- Cholesterol 0mg
- Sodium 480mg
- Carbs 30g
- Fibers 7g
- Sugars 8g
- Proteins 9g

Shopping List:

- Chickpeas
- Cauliflower
- Carrots
- Onion
- Garlic
- Ginger
- Cumin
- Turmeric
- Coconut milk
- Cilantro

Portobello Mushroom Burgers Grilled

These grilled Portobello mushroom burgers are an excellent vegetarian option for a main course. The portobello mushroom's succulent texture and earthy flavor make it an ideal substitute for meat patties.

Ingredients:

- 4 large packages of portobello mushrooms
- 2 tsp balsamic vinegar
- 2 tsp soy sauce
- 2 tsp olive oil
- 2 minced garlic cloves
- pepper and salt to flavor
- Burger patties
- Choose your toppings (lettuce, tomato, onion, cheese, etc.).

Preparation Guidelines:

1. Heat the grill (or barbecue) to a medium temperature.
2. Make a marinade using the balsamico, vinegar, olive oil, chopped garlic, salt and pepper in a shallow dish.
3. Remove stalks from Portobello caps, and add them to the marinade. Coat them thoroughly on both sides and marinate them for approximately 15 minutes.
4. Place the gill-side down of the marinated mushroom crowns on the preheated grill. Save the marinade for marinating the meat.
5. About 5-7 minutes per side, or until tender and marked with grill marks, grill the mushrooms. Baste the meat with the marinade from time to time during the barbecue.
6. Prepare the burger buns and garnishes while the mushrooms are grilling.
7. Toast the hamburger buns lightly on the grill or a griddle.
8. Place a mushroom cap on the bottom half of every bun to assemble the grilled portobello mushroom patties.
9. Add garnishes such as lettuce, tomato slices, onion, and cheese, if desired.
10. Place the upper portion of the bun atop the burger.
11. As a delicious vegetarian main course, serve the Portobello Mushroom Burgers immediately.
12. Add condiments such as ketchup, mustard, or mayonnaise to customize your burger.

Nutritional analysis per serving: (excluding baguette and toppings):

- Calories 120
- Fat 10g (1,5g Sat – 0g Trans)
- Cholesterol 0mg
- Sodium 530mg
- Carbs 6g
- Fibers 2g
- Sugars 3g
- Proteins 4g

Shopping List:

- Portobello mushroom caps
- Whole wheat hamburger buns
- Red onion
- Tomato
- Avocado
- Lettuce
- Balsamic vinegar
- Olive oil
- Garlic
- Dijon mustard

DESSERT RECIPES

Mixed Berry Parfait with Greek Yogurt

This Mixed Berry Parfait with Greek Yogurt is a healthy delicacy that combines the sweetness of mixed berries and the creaminess of Greek yogurt. Tasty but also rich in antioxidants and proteins.

Ingredients:

- 1 cup of assorted fruit (including strawberries, blueberries, and raspberries).
- 1 pint of Greek yogurt
- 2 tps honey maple syrup
- ¼ cup muesli
- Optional fresh mint sprigs for garnish

Preparation Guidelines:

1. The assorted berries are cleaned and patted dry. If using strawberries, remove and divide their stems.
2. In a bowl, thoroughly incorporate Greek yogurt and honey or maple syrup.
3. In serving glasses or dishes, layer the ingredients with a tablespoon of Greek yogurt.
4. Spread a layer of assorted berries over the yogurt.
5. Repeat the layers until all of the yogurt and berries have been used.
6. Granola should be sprinkled over the final layer of fruit.
7. If desirable, garnish with fresh mint leaves.
8. Serve the Mixed Berry Parfait immediately, or refrigerate for two hours to enable the flavors to combine.
9. Indulge guilt-free in the reviving and nutritious Mixed Berry Parfait.

Nutritional analysis per serving:

- Calories 180
- Fats 3g (1g Sat – 0g Trans)
- Cholesterol 10mg
- Sodium 40mg
- Carbs 32g
- Fibers 4g
- Sugars 21g
- Proteins 12g

Shopping List:

- Greek yogurt
- Mixed berries (fresh or frozen)
- Granola (look for a low-sugar option)
- Honey (optional)
- *Possible substitutions:*
- Use dairy-free yogurt alternative if preferred
- Use different types of fruit depending on your preference or what's in season
- Substitute granola for chopped nuts or toasted oats for a lower-carb option

Dark Chocolate Avocado Mousse

This Dark Chocolate Avocado Mousse is a decadent and creamy delicacy that combines the luxury of dark chocolate with the health benefits of avocado. It satisfies your chocolate appetite while providing beneficial nutrients and antioxidants.

Ingredients:

- 2 mature avocados
- ¼ cup powdered unsweetened cocoa
- ¼ cup almond milk (or milk)
- ¼ fluid ounce of maple nectar or honey
- 1 tsp vanilla extract
- A dash of salt
- Garnish with fresh berries or grated dark chocolate (optional).

Preparation Guidelines:

1. Cut the avocados into several pieces, and put everything in the blender (remove the stone)
2. Combine the cocoa powder, maple syrup or honey, milk, vanilla extract, and salt in a blender.
3. Blend until you get a creamy mixture.
4. You should taste the mousse and modify the sweetness or cocoa powder to your liking.
5. Place the Dark Chocolate Avocado Mousse in glasses or dishes for serving.
6. Allow the mousse to cool and set in the fridge for at least 1 hour.
7. If desired, garnish with fresh berries or shaved dark chocolate before serving.
8. As a gratifying dessert, indulge in the decadent and healthier Dark Chocolate Avocado Mousse.

Nutritional analysis per serving:

- Calories 200
- Fats14g (3g Sat. - 0 Trans)
- Cholesterol 0mg
- Sodium 20mg
- Carbs 21g
- Fibers 7g

Shopping List:

- Avocado
- Dark chocolate chips or cocoa powder
- Milk (dairy or non-dairy)
- Vanilla extract
- Salt

Possible substitutions:

- Use coconut milk instead of dairy milk for a vegan option
- Substitute maple syrup or honey for the sweetener
- Use carob chips instead of chocolate for a caffeine-free option

Apples baked with cinnamon and walnuts

Transforming fresh apples into a warm and flavorful dessert has never been easier, thanks to these Baked Apples with Cinnamon and Walnuts. This perfectly balanced recipe lets each ingredient shine - from the harmonious pairing of cinnamon with apples' innate sweetness right down to adding crisp texture through walnuts. Ideal for occasions ranging from cozy evenings at home to healthy alternatives at holiday gatherings - it's no wonder why this delicious treat has quickly become a household favorite!

Ingredients:

- Four apples of medium size (such as Granny Smith or Honeycrisp)
- 2 teaspoon honey or maple syrup
- 1 teaspoon cinnamon powder
- ¼ cup of ground walnuts
- 1 tablespoon unsalted butter, softened (optional)
- Greek yogurt or vanilla ice cream (optional)

Preparation Guidelines:

1. Preheat the oven to 375°F/190°.
2. Wash the apples and remove the cores.
3. Combine the maple syrup or honey and powdered cinnamon in a small bowl.
4. Using a pastry brush, place the apples in a baking dish and evenly coat them with the maple syrup or honey mixture.
5. Sprinkle chopped walnuts on each apple and delicately press them into the syrup mixture.
6. If desired, drizzle melted butter over the fruits to add a richer flavor.
7. Bake the apples for about 30 minutes in a oven or until tender and the walnuts are gently toasted.
8. Take them out and leave them to cool down for a few minutes.
9. Serve the warm Baked Apples with Cinnamon and Walnuts with a dollop of Greek yogurt or a serving of vanilla ice cream, if desired.

Nutritional analysis per serving: (no yogurt or ice cream):

- Calories 180
- Fats 6g (1g Sat – 0g Trans)
- Cholesterol 0mg
- Sodium 0mg
- Carbs 33g
- Fiber 6g
- Sugars 25g
- Proteins 2g

Shopping List:

- Apples
- Cinnamon
- Walnuts
- Honey or maple syrup (optional)

Possible substitutions:

- Use pecans or almonds instead of walnuts
- Substitute maple syrup or brown sugar for honey

Strawberry Chia Seed Pudding

Experience the delicious blend of natural strawberry sweetness and nutritional chia seed benefits with our Strawberry Chia Seed Pudding. This mouthwatering treat can be enjoyed for breakfast or as a guilt-free dessert option.

Ingredients:

1 fluid ounce of fresh strawberries

3 tbsp of chia

1 cup of unadulterated almond milk or any other nondairy milk.

½ tsp vanilla extract

1 tsp ful honey or maple syrup

Optional strawberries and mint sprigs for garnish

Preparation Guidelines:

1. If using frozen strawberries, they must be defrosted before continuing with the recipe.
2. In a blender, pulverize the strawberries until they are entirely smooth.
3. Combine the strawberry puree, almond milk, chia seeds, honey, and vanilla extract in a medium basin.
4. Let the chia seeds sit for about 5 minutes and stir to keep them from clumping.
5. For a pudding consistency, keep it in the fridge for at least 4 hours
6. Lumps may form after refrigeration; if so, stir again.
7. Pour the Strawberry Chia Seed Pudding into glasses or dishes for serving.
8. If desirable, garnish with fresh strawberries and mint leaves.
9. Serve the Strawberry Chia Seed Pudding chilled, and savor the delectable and wholesome dessert.

Nutritional analysis per serving:

- Calories 180
- Fats 7g (0,5g Sat – 0gTrans)
- Cholesterol 0mg
- Sodium 50mg
- Carbs 24g
- Fibers 9g
- Sugars 10g
- Proteins 5g

Shopping List:

- Chia seeds
- Milk (dairy or non-dairy)
- Strawberries
- Vanilla extract
- Honey or maple syrup (optional)

Possible substitutions:

- Use different types of berries or fruit depending on your preference or what's in season
- Substitute agave nectar or brown rice syrup for the sweetener

Banana Oat Cookies

Indulge in something sweet without compromising on your health goals with these Banana Oat Cookies. With their blend of ripe banana flavor and hearty oat texture these cookies deliver on both taste and nutrition in every bite.

Ingredients:

- 2 ripe bananas, pureed
- ¼ milligram cinnamon
- 1 pint of dried oats
- 2 tablespoons maple syrup or honey
- ¼ ounce of almond or peanut butter
- ½ tsp vanilla extract
- ¼ cup raisins or dark chocolate pieces (optional)

Preparation Guidelines:

1. Start by preheating your oven to 350°F/175°C while preparing a tray with baking paper to place inside once heated.
2. In a mixing bowl, combine thoroughly mashed bananas with rolled oats, nut butter (or almond butter), honey (or maple syrup), vanilla extract, and cinnamon to create a smooth mixture that is fragrant and flavorful.
3. To add a fun twist to your cookies, feel free to toss in some chocolate chips or raisins for a little extra sweetness and texture.
4. Arrange your cookie cutters onto the baking sheet before sliding them into the oven for around 12 to 15 minutes until you see those enticing golden edges. Once ready, let your biscuits cool down completely before storing them in an airtight container that lasts up to 3 to 4 days.

Nutritional analysis per serving: (1 cookie):

- Calories 90
- Fats 3g (0g Sat – 0g Trans)
- Cholesterol 0mg
- Sodium 0mg
- Carbs 14g
- Fibers 2g
- Sugars 6g
- Proteins 2g

Shopping List:

- Bananas
- Rolled oats
- Honey or maple syrup
- Cinnamon
- Salt

Possible substitutions:

- Use other types of fruit instead of bananas, such as applesauce or pumpkin puree
- Substitute agave nectar or brown rice syrup for the sweetener

Mixed Berry Sorbet

Satisfy your sweet tooth cravings with the tantalizing mixed berry blend found in this Sorbet recipe. Brimming with natural flavors that burst in your mouth this dessert perfectly complements sweltering heat conditions without compromising on nutrition content. The best part? With no dairy products included this recipe accommodates individuals who follow veganism or experience lactose sensitivities.

Ingredients:

- 2 cups fresh or frozen mixed fruit (such as raspberries, blueberries, and strawberries)
- ¼ fluid ounce of honey or maple syrup
- 1 tablespoon freshly strained lemon juice

Preparation Guidelines:

1. Place the assorted berries in a food processor or blender.
2. Honey or maple syrup and lemon juice should be added to the Vitamix.
3. Mix the ingredients at high speed until homogeneous and thoroughly combined.
4. If preferred, adjust the sweetness of the mixture by adding more honey or maple syrup.
5. Pour the berry mixture into a freezer-safe dish or container.
6. Cover the pan and freeze for about 4 hours, or until the sorbet has reached the desired consistency.
7. Removed from the freezer, let it soften for a few minutes at room temperature
8. Portion the sorbet into plates or glasses using a spoon or ice cream scoop.
9. Serve the Sorbet of Mixed Berries immediately and savor the burst of berry flavors.

Nutritional analysis per serving:

- Calories 80
- Fats 0g (0g Sat – 0g Trans)
- Cholesterol 0mg
- Sodium: 0mg
- Carbs 21g
- Fibers 3g
- Sugars 17g
- Proteins 0g

Shopping List:

- Mixed berries (fresh or frozen)
- Lemon juice
- Honey or agave nectar (optional)

Possible substitutions:

- Use different types of fruit depending on your preference or what's in season
- Substitute maple syrup or brown rice syrup for the sweetener

Blueberry Muffins with Almond Flour

With health conscious individuals in mind Almond Flour Blueberry Muffins offer a perfect solution without sacrificing taste. This gluten free recipe packs juicy blueberries into each delicious bite while using nutrient rich almond flour as the primary ingredient. These mouth watering muffins are suitable for speedy breakfasts or satisfying snacks that won't weigh you down.

Ingredients:

- 1 pound of almond flour
- ¼ cup coconut flour
- ½ tsp baking soda
- ¼ tsp salt
- 3 eggs
- ¼ fluid ounce of honey or maple syrup
- ¼ cup apple sauce unsweetened
- 1 tsp vanilla extract
- 1 fluid ounce of fresh or frozen blueberries

Preparation Guidelines:

1. First, preheat the oven to 350°C/175°C.
2. Line a muffin pan with cooking spray or parchment paper.
3. Whisk the almond flour, coconut flour, salt, and baking soda in a large mixing basin.
4. Whisk together the eggs, honey or maple syrup, applesauce, and vanilla extract in a separate basin.
5. Mix the liquid ingredients with the dry ones.
6. Fold in the blueberries with care.
7. Distribute the batter into the muffin cups, filling each approximately ¾ of the way.
8. Bake for 20 to 25 minutes.
9. Take the muffins out and cool them for 5 minutes.
10. The Almond Flour Blueberry Muffins are a delicious and nutritious snack.

Analysis of nutrition per serving (1 muffin):

- Calories 160
- Fats11g (1g Sat – 0g Trans)
- Sodium 110mg
- Carbs 13g
- Fiber 3g
- Sugars 8g
- Proteins 5g

Shopping List:

- Almond flour
- Baking powder
- Salt
- Eggs
- Honey or maple syrup
- Vanilla extract
- Blueberries

Popsicles with Greek Yogurt and Fresh Fruit

Craving something sweet but don't want to compromise on health? Treat yourself to these delightful Greek Yogurt Popsicles with Fresh Fruit! Made from tangy Greek yogurt and chunks of fresh colorful fruits they're effortless to prepare and sure to please any palate. Whether you need to cool off on a sultry afternoon or unwind after dinner they hit the spot every time.

Ingredients:

- ½cup of fresh mixed fruit (including strawberries, raspberries, and blueberries).
- 1 pint of Greek yogurt
- ½ cup of raw pineapple dice
- ½ cup of mango, minced
- honey, 1 to 2 teaspoons (optional)
- Molds for popsicles and skewers

Preparation Guidelines:

1. Blend fresh mixed berries and Greek yogurt until they reach an irresistible smoothness for your tastebuds!
2. In another blender or food processor, puree together diced pineapple and mango pieces separately to create more fruity goodness! Remember to add some honey if you like it sweeter!
3. Pour half your creamy mix into each mold before topping them off with your vibrant fruit blend!
4. Carefully use your spoon or popsicle stick to create swirly designs within it all before sticking in one last time and allowing them to freeze up well for at least four hours!
5. Once the popsicles are frozen, run them briefly under warm water to extricate them from the molds.
6. Serve the Greek Yogurt Popsicles with Fresh Fruit immediately and savor this nutritious and refreshing delicacy.

Nutritional analysis per serving:

- Calories 80
- Fats 0g (0g Sat – 0g Trans)
- Cholesterol 0mg
- Sodium 10mg
- Carbs 18g
- Fibers 2g
- Sugars 14g
- Proteins 3g

Shopping List:

- Greek yogurt
- Milk (dairy or non-dairy)
- Honey
- Vanilla extract
- Fresh fruit (such as berries, kiwi, or mango)

Possible substitutions:

- Use different types of fruit depending on your preference or what's in season
- Substitute maple syrup or brown rice syrup for the sweetener

Coconut and Dark Chocolate Energy Balls

Satisfy your hunger pangs with these scrumptious Coconut and Dark Chocolate Energy Balls - bursting with wholesome goodness! Jam packed with nutrient dense ingredients such as shredded coconut flakes, almond flour, dark chocolate bits or cocoa powder (depending on preference) plus natural sweeteners like dates or honey - they offer a healthy alternative to traditional snacks. Whether you need fuel before a workout or just want to indulge in something deliciously guilt free throughout the day - make sure to give them a try!

Ingredients:

- 1 cup desiccated coconut flakes
- 1 tablespoon almond flour
- ¼ cup dark chocolate pieces (at least 70% cocoa)
- 2 tps maple syrup or honey
- 2 tps of almond spread
- ½ tsp vanilla extract
- A dash of salt

Preparation Guidelines:

1. Combine the shredded coconut, almond flour, dark chocolate chips, and salt in a mixing basin.
2. In a small bowl, mix the honey, butter, and vanilla extract
3. Pour the mixture into the dry ingredients and thoroughly combine until the mixture is glutinous and cohesive.
4. Add almond butter or honey if the mix is too dry.
5. With your hands make balls about 1 inch in diameter with the mixture
6. Place the energy spheres on an aluminum foil-lined baking sheet.
7. Refrigerate the energy spheres for at least thirty minutes to harden them.
8. After being refrigerated, the Coconut and Dark Chocolate Energy Balls are available for consumption.
9. Refrigerate any remaining energy spheres in an airtight container for up to one week.

Nutritional Analysis for two energy spheres per serving:

- Calories 140
- Fats 11g (6g Sat – 0g Trans)
- Cholesterol 0mg
- Sodium 10mg
- Carbs 10g
- Fibers 3g
- Sugars 6g
- Proteins 3g

Shopping List:

- Dates
- Coconut flakes
- Almond flour
- Dark chocolate chips or cocoa powder
- Vanilla extract

Possible substitutions:

- Use different types of nuts, such as pecans or cashews, instead of almond flour
- Substitute carob chips for the chocolate
- Use other types of dried fruit instead of dates, such as figs or apricots

BEVERAGES RECIPES

Green Smoothie Recipe with Spinach and Pineapple

Start your day right or replenish your energy after a workout with this refreshing and nutritious Green Smoothie thats brimming with vitamins and minerals. The vibrant green color comes from fresh spinach and sweet pineapple along with other nourishing ingredients. Its both delicious and nutritious making it the perfect beverage to fuel your body.

Ingredients:
- 2 cups of fresh spinach
- 1 cup diced pineapple
- 1 mature banana
- ½ cup unadulterated almond milk (or your preferred milk)
- 1 teaspoon honey or maple syrup (optional for additional sweetener)
- ½ cup ice chunks

Preparation Guidelines:
1. Blend the fresh spinach leaves, pineapple cubes, mature banana, unsweetened almond milk, and honey or maple syrup, if desired, until the consistency is smooth and creamy.
2. Add ice until the smoothie is chilled and foamy.
3. Serve the Green Smoothie immediately by pouring it into glasses.
4. You may garnish the smoothie with a pineapple slice and chia seeds if preferred.

Nutritional analysis per serving:
- Calories 160
- Fats 1g (og Sat – 0g Trans)
- Cholesterol 0mg
- Sodium: 60mg
- Carbs 39g
- Fibers 5g
- Sugar:s 24g
- Proteins 3g

Shopping List:
- Fresh spinach leaves
- Pineapple
- Banana
- Almond milk (unsweetened)

Possibke substitutions:
- Kale or arugula can be substituted for spinach
- Mango or peach can be substituted for pineapple
- Greek yogurt can be substituted for banana for added protein

Raspberry Iced Tea

Indulge in a refreshing drink that blends together two delicious flavors - tea and raspberry - into one enticing sip. When made from scratch at home Raspberry Iced Tea lets you experiment with different levels of sweetness and tartness until you achieve your desired balance.

Ingredients:

- 4 gallons water
- Four raspberry tea leaves
- 1 ounce of ripe raspberries
- 1-2 teaspoons honey or agave syrup (optional for additional flavor)
- Ice crystals
- Optional fresh mint sprigs for garnish

Preparation Guidelines:

1. Boil some water in a pot.
2. Add the tea bags after removing the pot from the heat.
3. Strain the tea for five to seven minutes to infuse the flavors.
4. Remove and discard the tea sachets from the saucepan.
5. Fresh raspberries should be added to the tea and infused for 10 minutes.
6. Using a spatula, crush the raspberries in the tea to extract their juices.
7. Add honey or agave syrup, if desirable, to sweeten the iced tea. Begin with one tablespoon and adjust to flavor.
8. Pour the tea into a pitcher.
9. Chill the carafe of tea in the refrigerator.
10. Fill glasses with ice and pour tea and serve them.
11. If desirable, garnish with fresh mint leaves.
12. Stir before drinking and savor the flavorful refreshment.

Nutritional analysis per serving:

- Calories 15
- Fats 0g (0g Sat – 0g Trans)
- Cholesterol 0mg
- Sodium 5mg
- Carbs 4g
- Fibers 1g
- Sugars 3g
- Proteins 0g

Shopping List:

- Black tea bags
- Fresh raspberries
- Lemon juice
- Honey (optional)
- Water

Possible substitutions:

- Green tea bags can be substituted for black tea bags
- Frozen raspberries can be substituted for fresh raspberries
- Maple syrup can be substituted for honey for a vegan option

Citrus Detox Water

Citrus Detox Water is a refreshing and hydrating beverage that aids in cleansing and revitalizing the body. By infusing water with citrus fruits such as lemon, lime, and orange, you can experience a healthy and refreshing beverage.

Ingredients:

- 4 gallons water
- 1 citrus fruit, cut
- 1 lime, cut
- 1 tangerine, segmented
- Mint leaves, fresh (optional)
- Ice crystals

Preparation Guidelines:

1. Combine the water, lemon, lime, and orange slices in a pitcher.
2. If desirable, add fresh mint leaves for an additional flavor boost.
3. To distribute the flavors, mix the ingredients gently.
4. For a more robust flavor, leave the jug in the refrigerator for about an hour, preferably overnight.
5. When serving, fill the glasses with ice crystals.
6. Include fruit slices when pouring the Citrus Detox Water into the vessels and including fruit slices.
7. Stir and appreciate the drink's reviving and detoxifying properties.

Analysis of nutrition per serving:

- Calories 5
- Fats 0g (0g Sat – 0g Trans)
- Cholesterol 0mg
- Sodium 0mg
- Carbs 2g
- Fibers 1g
- Sugars 1g
- Proteins 0g

Shopping List:

- Lemon
- Lime
- Orange
- Cucumber
- Mint leaves
- Water

Carrot and radish juice

For a revitalizing yet nutrient packed beverage try Beetroot and Carrot Juice! This delectable elixir brims with antioxidants, vitamins, and minerals that contribute to your wellness. Not only does it enhance digestion by supporting a healthy gut microbiome but also promotes overall health by supplying vital nutrients to the body.

Ingredients:

- 2 beets of medium size, peeled and sliced
- 1 tiny lemon, peeled
- 1-inch hunk of peeled ginger
- 4 carrots, peeled and diced, medium size
- 1-2 teaspoons honey or agave syrup (optional for additional flavor)
- Ice crystals (if desired).

Preparation Guidelines:

1. Chop the beets, carrots, ginger, and lemon and place them in a juicer.
2. Utilizing a juicer, process the ingredients to extract all of the liquid.
3. Add honey to sweeten the juice, if desired. Begin with one tablespoon and adjust to flavor.
4. Mix the juice thoroughly to combine its flavors.
5. Fill glasses with Beetroot and Carrot Juice.
6. If desired, add ice crystals to the drinks to chill the liquid.
7. Stir before consuming and savor the nutritious and vibrant beverage.

Nutritional analysis per serving:

- Calories 80
- Fats 0g (0g Sat – 0g Trans)
- Cholesterol 0mg
- Sodium 100mg
- Carbs 20g
- Fibers 4g
- Sugars 14g
- Proteins 2g

Shopping List:

- Beetroot
- Carrot
- Apple
- Ginger
- Lemon juice
- Water

Possible substitutions:

- Pear can be substituted for apple
- Turmeric can be substituted for ginger
- Coconut water can be substituted for water for added electrolytes

Matcha Green Tea Latte

Its time to treat yourself to something truly decadent - introducing the Matcha Green Tea Latte! The blend of matcha tea powder and milk creates an unbeatable smoothness that will satisfy your cravings while also providing numerous health benefits. Brimming with antioxidants and offering mild energy boosting effects this latte is simply heavenly. Don't wait any longer- indulge yourself today!

Ingredients:

- 1 teaspoon powdered matcha
- 2 teaspoons warm water
- 1 cup milk (of any variety, including almond milk, soy milk, and cow's milk)
- 1-2 tablespoons honey or maple syrup (optional for sweetening)

Preparation Guidelines:

1. Whisk matcha powder and hot water in a basin until no lumps remain, and the matcha powder has dissolved.
2. Heat the milk without boiling it.
3. Pour it into the matcha mixture in the basin.
4. Add honey or maple syrup, if desirable, to sweeten the latte. Start with 1 teaspoon and adjust to flavor as necessary.
5. Whisk the matcha mixture and milk until frothy and thoroughly blended.
6. Warm the Matcha Green Tea Latte and pour it into a cup.

Nutritional analysis per serving:

- Calories 80
- Fats 3g (2g Sat – 0g Trans)
- Cholesterol 12 mg
- Sodium 10mg
- Carbs 10g
- Fibers 1g
- Sugars 9g
- Proteins 5g

Shopping List:

- Matcha powder
- Almond milk (unsweetened)
- Honey (optional)

Possible substitutions:

- Soy milk or coconut milk can be substituted for almond milk
- Agave nectar can be substituted for honey for a vegan option

Blueberry Banana Smoothie

Savor the taste of Blueberry Banana Smoothie – an alluring blend of ripe bananas infused with blueberries brimming full of antioxidants. Loaded with crucial vitamins, minerals, and fiber that enhance its nutritional quotient significantly; this smoothie isn't just refreshing but also serves as an excellent option to start your day or take as a wholesome snack.

Ingredients:

- 1 mature banana
- 1 fluid ounce blueberries
- 1 cup unadulterated almond milk (or your preferred milk)
- 1 teaspoon honey or maple syrup (optional for additional sweetener)
- ½ teaspoon vanilla extract
- If utilizing fresh blueberries, add ice crystals.

Preparation Guidelines:

1. Combine the banana, blueberries, almond milk, honey, maple syrup (if using), and vanilla extract in a Vitamix.
2. Add a handful of ice crystals to the blender for a chilled smoothie made with fresh blueberries.
3. Combine the ingredients until velvety and smooth.
4. If the texture is too dense, add almond milk and blend again.
5. If desired, add more honey or maple syrup to modify the smoothie's sweetness.
6. The Blueberry Banana Smoothie should be poured into glasses.
7. Enjoy the revitalizing flavors and nutritional benefits of this smoothie as soon as possible.

Nutritional analysis per serving:

- Calories 150
- Fats 2g (0g Sat – 0g Trans)
- Cholesterol 0mg
- Sodium 100mg
- Carbs 34g
- Fibers 5g
- Sugars 20g
- Proteins 2g

Shopping List:

- Fresh blueberries
- Banana
- Greek yogurt
- Almond milk (unsweetened)

Possible substitutions:

- Frozen blueberries can be substituted for fresh blueberries
- Peanut butter can be added for extra protein
- Soy milk or coconut milk can be substituted for almond milk

Cucumber and Mint Infused Water

Cucumber Mint Infused Water is a refreshing and hydrating beverage with a hint of natural flavoring added to ordinary water. This infused water is ideal for staying hydrated throughout the day, thanks to the subtle calming effect of mint and the crispness of cucumber. Extremely straightforward to make and a healthy alternative to sugary beverages.

Ingredients:

- 8 pints water
- 1 medium cucumber, cut
- 10 to 12 mint sprigs
- Ice crystals

Preparation Guidelines:

1. Add the water to the pitcher.
2. Cucumber segments and mint leaves should be added to the pitcher.
3. Cucumber and mint are muddled with a wooden spoon to unleash their flavors.
4. For best flavor place the pitcher in the refrigerator for at least 2 hours.
5. When serving, fill the glasses with ice crystals.
6. Include cucumber slices and mint fronds when pouring the Cucumber Mint Infused Water into glasses.
7. Stir and savor this water's crisp and revitalizing flavor.

Nutritional analysis per serving:

- Calories 0
- Fats 0g (0g Sat – 0g Trans)
- Cholesterol 0mg
- Sodium 10mg
- Carbs 0g
- Fibers 0g
- Sugars 0g
- Protein 0g

Shopping List:

- Cucumber
- Mint leaves
- Water

Possible substitutions:

- Lemon or lime slices can be added for a citrus flavor
- Basil leaves can be substituted for mint leaves

Homemade Lemonade with Stevia

Don't let sweltering days leave you parched and dehydrated; try homemade lemonade with Stevia instead! Its crisp taste and ability to quench your thirst make it the perfect summer beverage. By replacing artificial sweeteners with Stevia - natures sweetheart - this recipe slashes calories and sugar content significantly.

Ingredients:

- 4-5 large lemons, juiced (approximately 1 cup of lemon juice)
- 4 gallons water
- ¼ cup of stevia (adjust to flavor).
- Ice crystals
- Optional lemon wedges for garnish

Preparation Guidelines:

1. When life gives you lemons (and some sweetener), why not make homemade lemonade?
2. Start by combining freshly strained lemon juice with some water in a pitcher, along with just enough stevia to bring out that natural tartness.
3. Stir everything together well so that the sweetness and tartness are evenly distributed throughout the mixture.
4. Adjust according to taste preferences by adding more sweetening if necessary before filling up your glasses or containers with plenty of ice cubes (colder drinks are always better).

Nutritional analysis per serving:

- Calories 10
- Fats 0g (0g Sat- 0gTrans)
- Cholesterol 0mg
- Sodium 0mg
- Carbs 3g
- Fibers 0g
- Sugars 0g
- Proteins 0g

Shopping List:

- Lemon juice
- Stevia
- Water

Possble substitutions:

- Lime juice can be added for a citrus twist
- Honey or agave nectar can be substituted for stevia

Mango Lassi (Yogurt Smoothie)

The tropical flavor of mango inside a yogurt. This refreshing drink is not only delectable but also provides probiotics and vitamins from yogurt and mangoes. Whether consumed as a refreshing beverage or a gratifying dessert, the Mango Lassi is sure to please the palate.

Ingredients:

- 1 mango, peeled, seeded, and chopped when mature
- 1 pint of basic yogurt
- ½ cup milk (any variety, including almond milk or cow's milk)
- 1 teaspoon honey or maple syrup (optional for additional sweetener)
- optional ¼ teaspoon ground cardamom
- Ice crystals (if desired).

Preparation Guidelines:

1. Blend the diced mango, plain yogurt, milk, honey, or maple syrup (if using), and cardamom powder (if using) in a blender.
2. If you desire a chilled smoothie, add a handful of ice crystals to the blender.
3. Combine the ingredients until velvety and smooth.
4. If preferred, adjust the sweetness of the Mango Lassi by adding more honey or maple syrup.
5. The smoothie is poured into glasses.
6. Serve immediately and savor the pleasant tropical flavors of this Mango Lassi.

Nutritional analysis per serving:

- Calories 180
- Fats 4g (2g Sat – 0g Trans)
- Cholesterol 15mg/ml
- Sodium 80mg
- Carbs 32g
- Fibers 2g
- Sugar:s 8g
- Proteins 7g

Shopping List

- Mango
- Greek yogurt
- Almond milk (unsweetened)
- Cardamom powder

Possible substitutions:

- Coconut yogurt can be substituted for Greek yogurt for a vegan option
- Cashew milk can be substituted for almond milk

SALAD RECIPES

Quinoa Salad with Roasted Vegetables

If you're after a delicious yet health-packed salad option - why not try out the Quinoa Salad with Roasted Vegetables? This delectable medley intertwines the unique nuttiness of quinoa with beautifully prepared roasted veggies producing an irresistible fusion that will leave your taste buds yearning for more. This salad offers undeniable tastiness and provides excellent nutritional value by delivering essential fiber and the necessary vitamins and minerals vital for your overall health. Thanks to its remarkable roasted veggie flavors intertwined within its protein-rich quinoa base, this dish can stand alone as a refreshing brunch option or even be enjoyed as an indulgent side dish to any dinner feast.

Ingredients:

- 1 small eggplant, minced
- 2 cups liquid, either water or bouillon
- 1 minced yellow bell pepper
- 1 zucchini, sliced
- 1 minced red bell pepper
- ¼ cup fresh minced parsley
- 1 red onion, cut thinly
- 2 tsp olive oil
- 1 cup quinoa
- 1 teaspoon rosemary leaves
- Lemon juice extracted from one lemon
- pepper and salt to flavor
- Optional garnishes include feta cheese crumbles and sliced almonds.

Preparation Guidelines:

1. Drain the quinoa after rinsing it with cool water.
2. Put the quinoa in a saucepan with water or broth and bring to a boil, then cook for another 15 minutes (the quinoa must be tender and the water absorbed), cover with a lid, and reduce the heat. Remove and allow to cool.
3. Spread eggplant, zucchini, bell peppers, and onion on a baking sheet. Drizzle olive oil and sprinkle dried thyme, salt, and pepper on the vegetables. To uniformly coat the vegetables, toss them.
4. Roast in preheated oven at 425°F/220°C for about 25 minutes or until tender and lightly browned. The vegetables must be stirred midway through cooking.
5. Combine the cooked quinoa and caramelized vegetables in a large bowl. Combine chopped cilantro with lemon juice. Toss to mix thoroughly.
6. Season to taste with salt and pepper.
7. The Quinoa Salad with Roasted Vegetables should be served at room temperature or chilled.
8. Add flavor and texture by topping with crumbled feta cheese and sliced hazelnuts, if desired.

Nutrition analysis per serving

- Calories 280
- Fats 10g (1g Sat – 0g Trans)
- Cholesterol 0mg
- Sodium 30mg
- Carbs 42g
- Fibers 7g
- Sugars 7g
- Proteins 8g

Shopping List:

- Quinoa
- Assorted Vegetables (such as bell peppers, zucchini, eggplant, carrots, etc.)
- Olive Oil
- Salt and Pepper
- Lemon Juice
- Garlic

Possible substitutions:

You can replace quinoa with brown rice or barley. Use vegetables you like or have on hand. Herbs and spices like thyme or rosemary can be added to make it more aromatic.

Greek Salad with Feta and Olives

Treat your senses to an explosion of flavors by relishing in one of Greece's most well-crafted dishes - The Greek Salad With Feta And Olives - That will astound any food enthusiast. This classic Mediterranean masterpiece is composed of crisp veggies imbued with zestiness presented alongside tantalizing feta cheese crumbles interlaced with piquant saltiness from the olives tossed together in lip-smacking vinaigrette. This wholesome salad's richness caters to health-conscious individuals' preference, making it an appropriate choice as a light meal or side dish that refreshes your taste buds for any occasion.

Ingredients:

- Four cups of assorted salad greens (like romaine lettuce, arugula, or spinach).
- 1 cup halved cherry tomatoes
- 1 cucumber sliced into rings
- ½ red scallion, sliced thinly
- ½ cup Kalamata olives, pitted
- ½cup of shredded feta
- 1 gram of red wine vinegar
- 2 tsp extra virgin olive oil
- 1 tsp powdered dried oregano
- salt and pepper to flavor

Preparation Guidelines:

1. Combine the mixed salad greens, cherry tomatoes, diced cucumber, red onion slices, Kalamata olives, and crumbled feta cheese.
2. To make the dressing, mix the extra virgin olive oil, dried oregano, red wine vinegar, salt and pepper.
3. Drizzle the dressing in the the salad, then gently toss to coat the ingredients adequately.
4. You can adjust the salad's seasoning with additional salt and pepper if you wish, then serve.

Nutrition analysis per serving

- Calories: 180
- Fats 14g (4g Sat – 0g Trans)
- Cholesterol 15 mg
- Sodium 400mg
- Carbs 9g
- Fibers 3g
- Sugars 4g
- Proteins 5g

Shopping List:

- Tomatoes
- Cucumbers
- Red Onion
- Lemon Juice
- Olive Oil
- Feta Cheese
- Kalamata Olives
- Salt and Pepper
- Dried Oregano

Possible substitutions:

Add greens, such lettuce or celery, to the salad. To make it vegan, replace the feta with tofu or chickpeas.

Strawberry and Spinach Salad with Balsamic Vinaigrette

Spinach and Strawberry Salad with Balsamic Vinaigrette is a delectable blend of fresh spinach leaves, juicy strawberries, and crunchy almonds. Not only is this salad visually enticing, but it is also bursting with flavor and texture. The sweetness of the strawberries and the balsamic vinaigrette's tartness complements the spinach's earthiness.

Ingredients:

- 4 cups of fresh infant spinach
- 1 cup cut and hulled strawberries
- 1 teaspoon Dijon mustard
- Optional: 2 teaspoons of crumbled feta cheese
- For the Balsamic Vinaigrette, combine the following ingredients:
- 3 tablespoons extra virgin olive oil
- 1 teaspoonful vinegar
- ¼ cup almonds cut
- 1 milligram of honey
- pepper and salt to flavor

Preparation Guidelines:

1. Fresh baby spinach leaves, sliced strawberries, sliced almonds, and crumbled feta cheese (if using) are combined in a large salad bowl.
2. To prepare the balsamic vinaigrette, combine the oil, balsamic vinegar, Dijon mustard, honey, salt, and pepper in a separate small bowl.
3. Drizzle the vinaigrette in the salad and toss gently to coat.
4. Adjust the salad's seasonings and vinaigrette to taste.
5. Serve the Spinach and Strawberry Salad with Balsamic Vinaigrette as a light, refreshing main course or side dish.

Nutrition analysis per serving:

- Calories: 180
- Fats 15g (2g Sat – 0g Trans)
- Cholesterol 2mg
- Sodium 150mg
- Carbs 9g
- Fibers 3g
- Sugars 5g
- Proteins 4g

Shopping List:

- Baby Spinach
- Strawberries
- Red Onion
- Almonds
- Balsamic Vinegar
- Olive Oil
- Honey
- Dijon Mustard

Possible substitutions:

Other berries, such as blueberries or raspberries, can be used. You can also substitute pecans or walnuts for the almonds.

Arugula, Pear, and Walnut Salad

Arugula, Pear, and Walnut Salad is a delectable blend of peppery arugula, sweet and juicy pears, and crunchy walnuts. This salad, tossed in a light lemon vinaigrette, is a refreshing and gratifying combination of flavors.

Ingredients:

- 4 tablespoons arugula
- 2 ripe pears, cut
- ½ cup roughly minced walnuts
- ¼cup goat cheese crumbles (optional).
- For the Lemon Vinaigrette, combine:
- 3 tbsp olive oil
- 1 teaspoonful lemon juice
- 1 tsp Dijon mustard
- 1 milligram of honey
- pepper and salt to flavor

Preparation Guidelines:

1. Combine the arugula, sliced pears, minced walnuts, and crumbled goat cheese (if using).
2. Make a vinaigrette by mixing the oil, fresh lemon juice, honey, mustard, salt, and pepper.
3. Pour the vinaigrette over salad.
4. Taste the salad and modify the seasoning or vinaigrette to your liking.
5. Serve the Arugula, Pear, and Walnut Salad as a side dish with grilled chicken or seafood or as a refreshing salad on its own.

Nutritional analysis per serving:

- Calories: 200
- Fats 16g (2g Sat – 0g Trans)
- Cholesterol 0mg
- Sodium 100mg
- Carbs14g
- Fibers 4g
- Sugars 8g
- Proteins 4g

Shopping List:

- Arugula
- Pears
- Walnuts
- Blue Cheese
- Olive Oil
- Lemon Juice
- Salt and Pepper

Possible substitutions:

Instead of walnuts, you can use almonds or pistachios. It is even possible to replace the blue cheese with goat's cheese.

Caprese Salad with Fresh Basil

Instead of walnuts, you can use almonds or pistachios. It is even possible to replace the blue cheese with goat's cheese. Caprese Salad is an Italian dish highlighting the vibrant flavors of succulent tomatoes, fresh mozzarella cheese, and aromatic basil leaves. It features the tomatoes' natural richness and the mozzarella's creamy texture. This Caprese salad, drizzled with extra virgin olive oil and balsamic glaze, is an ideal appetizer or side dish for any entrée.

Ingredients:

- Four mature tomatoes, sliced;
- eight ounces of fresh mozzarella, sliced
- Basil fronds grown from the ground
- Extra virgin olive oil, for pouring
- Balsamic glaze, for sprinkling
- pepper and salt to flavor

Preparation Guidelines:

1. On a serving platter, alternate the tomatoes with the mozzarella.
2. Layer tomato and mozzarella slices with fresh basil leaves.
3. The Caprese salad should be drizzled with oil and balsamic vinaigrette.
4. Add salt and pepper.
5. Serve

Nutritional analysis per serving:

- Calories: 250
- Fats 18g (8g Sat – 0g Trans)
- Cholesterol 40 mg
- Sodium 350mg
- Carbs 5g
- Fibers 1g
- Sugars 3g
- Proteins 16g

Shopping List:

- Tomatoes
- Fresh Mozzarella Cheese
- Fresh Basil
- Balsamic Vinegar
- Olive Oil
- Salt and Pepper

Possible substitutions:

You can add other vegetables, such as cucumbers or bell peppers, to the salad. If you want the vegan version, you can replace the mozzarella cheese with tofu or avocado.

Quinoa and Kale Salad with Lemon Dressing

Kale and Quinoa Salad with Lemon Dressing is a healthy and satisfying salad that combines the earthy flavors of kale and quinoa with the vibrant and zesty taste of lemon. Packed with vitamins, minerals, and protein, the salad makes an excellent light lunch or side dish. The lemon dressing enhances the dish's overall flavor with its refreshing acidity.

Ingredients:

- 4 cups minced, de-stemmed kale leaves
- 1 cup prepared quinoa
- ¼cup almonds cut
- ¼measure of dried blackberries
- 2 teaspoons freshly squeezed lemon juice
- 1 milligram of honey
- 1 tsp Dijon mustard
- 2 teaspoons extra virgin olive oil
- Salt and pepper

Preparation Guidelines:

1. Combine the diced kale, cooked quinoa, sliced almonds, and dried cranberries.
2. Make the lemon dressing by combining the lemon juice, oil, mustard, honey, salt, and pepper.
3. Sprinkle with vinaigrette and toss to coat.
4. Permit the salad to remain for a few minutes so the flavors can combine.
5. As a nutritious and vibrant salad, serve the Kale and Quinoa Salad with Lemon Dressing.

Nutritional analysis per serving:

- Calories: 250
- Fats 12g (1g Sat – 0 Trans)
- Cholesterol 0mg
- Sodium 150mg
- Carbs 30g
- Fibers 5g
- Sugars 6g
- Proteins 8g

Shopping List:

- Kale
- Quinoa
- Chickpeas
- Carrots
- Red Onion
- Lemon Juice
- Olive Oil
- Honey
- Dijon Mustard

Possible substitutions:

Any other bean, such as black beans or kidney beans, can replace chickpeas. To make it vegan, you can also replace the honey with maple syrup.

Watermelon Feta Salad with Mint

Combining the flavors of watermelon, feta cheese, and mint leaves, Watermelon Feta Salad with Mint is a refreshing and light salad. This salad is ideal for the summer because of its hydrating seasonings.

Ingredients:

- 4 cups cubed, seedless cantaloupe
- ½ cup of shredded feta
- ¼ cup minced fresh mint leaves
- 1 teaspoonful extra virgin olive oil
- 1 teaspoonful balsamic glaze
- pepper and salt to flavor

Preparation Guidelines:

1. Combine watermelon cubes, crumbled feta cheese, and minced mint leaves.
2. Drizzle the salad with the oil and balsamic glaze.
3. Season with salt and pepper
4. Toss the ingredients together gently
5. Before serving, allow the Watermelon Feta Salad with Mint to marinate in the refrigerator for approximately 15 minutes.

Nutritional analysis per serving:

- Calories: 120
- Fats 5g (2g Sat – 0g Trans)
- Cholesterol 10 milligrams
- Sodium 200mg
- Carbs 15g
- Fibers 1g
- Sugars 12g
- Proteins 4g

Shopping List:

- Watermelon
- Feta Cheese
- Fresh Mint
- Balsamic Vinegar
- Olive Oil
- Salt and Pepper

Possible substitutions:

You can also add strawberries or blueberries. It can be made vegan with tofu or avocado.

Citrus-dressed beet and goat cheese salad

The vibrant and flavorful Beet and Goat Cheese Salad with Citrus Dressing combines roasted beets' earthy sweetness with goat cheese's piquant creaminess. This salad, tossed in a citrus-based dressing, is a delectable combination of flavors.

Ingredients:

- 3 roasted and thinly sliced medium beets
- 4 cups assorted salad greens
- ¼ cup of ground walnuts
- ½cup goat cheese crumbs
- 1 tbsp freshly strained lemon juice
- 2 teaspoons freshly squeezed orange juice
- oil 1 milligram of honey
- 2 teaspoons extra virgin olive
- pepper and salt to flavor

Preparation Guidelines:

1. Arrange the assorted salad greens according to the preparation instructions.
2. Add to salad greens, add the sliced roasted beets, crumbled goat cheese, and minced walnuts.
3. Mix fresh lemon juice, orange juice, oil, honey, salt, and pepper.
4. Over the salad, pour the vinaigrette and toss gently to coat.
5. Before serving, let the Beet and Goat Cheese Salad with Citrus Dressing settle for a few minutes to allow the flavors to meld.

Nutritional analysis per serving:

- Calories: 180
- Fats 12g (4g Sat – 0g Trans)
- Cholesterol 10 mg
- Sodium 200mg
- Carbs 15g
- Fibers 4g
- Sugars 9g
- Proteins 6g

Shopping List:

- Beets
- Goat Cheese
- Walnuts
- Arugula
- Orange Juice
- Olive Oil
- Dijon Mustard
- Honey

Possible substitutions:

You can substitute other nuts like pecan or almond. You can also substitute maple syrup for vegan honey.

Avocado Salad with Lime-Cilantro Dressing

Mango Avocado Salad with Lime-Cilantro Dressing is a revitalizing and tropical salad that combines the juiciness and richness of mangoes and avocados with the zesty flavors of lime and cilantro. This salad is a kaleidoscope of colors and flavors, making it a great option for the summer or whenever you're craving a light and revitalizing meal.

Ingredients:

- 2 avocados, peeled and sliced, ripe
- 2 mature mangoes, peeled and diced
- ½ red scallion, sliced thinly
- ¼ cup fresh chopped coriander
- 2 teaspoons extra virgin olive oil
- The juice of two limes
- 1 milligram of honey
- pepper and salt to flavor

Preparation Guidelines:

1. Combine diced mangoes, diced avocados, sliced red onion, and fresh minced cilantro in a large salad bowl.
2. Combine lime juice, extra virgin olive oil, honey, salt, and pepper to prepare the lime-cilantro dressing.
3. Drizzle the lime-cilantro dressing over the salad and gently swirl to combine.
4. Allow the flavors in the Mango Avocado Salad with Lime-Cilantro Dressing to meld for a few minutes.
5. Serve the salad as a refreshing and tropical side dish or as a light and filling entrée.

Nutritional analysis per serving:

- Calories: 220
- Fats 16g (2g Sat – 0 Trans)
- Cholesterol 0mg
- Sodium 100mg
- Carbs 20g
- Fibers 8g
- Sugars 10g
- Proteins 3g

Shopping List:

- Mango
- Red Onion
- Avocado
- Olive Oil
- Lime Juice
- Cilantro
- Honey
- Salt and Pepper

Cucumber, Tomato, and Avocado Salad

The Cucumber, Tomato, and Avocado Salad is a revitalizing salad highlighting the natural flavors of crisp cucumbers, juicy tomatoes, and creamy avocados.

Ingredients:

- 2 peeled and cut cucumbers
- 1/4 cup thinly sliced red onion
- 2 diced tomatoes 1 diced avocado
- juice 2 teaspoons extra virgin olive oil
- 2 teaspoons freshly squeezed lemon
- 1 tablespoon fresh chopped dill
- pepper and salt to flavor

Preparation Guidelines:

1. Combine the sliced cucumbers, tomatoes, avocado, and sliced red onion in a large salad bowl.
2. To prepare the dressing, combine lemon juice, extra virgin olive oil, chopped fresh dill, salt, and pepper in a small bowl.
3. Drizzle the vinaigrette in the salad.
4. Allow the Cucumber, Tomato, and Avocado Salad to rest for a few minutes to combine the flavors.
5. Serve the salad as a light, nutritious side dish or a healthy lunch option.

Nutritional analysis per serving:

- Calories: 150
- Fats 12g (2g Sat – 0g Trans)
- Cholesterol 0mg
- Sodium 20mg
- Carbs 11g
- Fibers 6g
- Sugars 4g
- Proteins 2g

Shopping List:

- Red onion
- Cucumber
- Tomatoes
- Avocado
- Olive oil
- Lime juice
- Cilantro
- Salt and black pepper

Possible substitutions:

Instead of cilantro, you can use parsley or basil. You can add some feta cheese or queso fresco for extra flavor. Use lemon juice if you don't have lime juice.

SOUP RECIPES

Tomato Basil Soup served with Whole Wheat Bread

Tomato Basil broth with Whole Wheat Bread is a traditional and comforting broth that combines the rich flavors of tomatoes and fragrant basil. This broth, served with a side of hearty whole wheat bread, is a satisfying and nutritious option for a meal.

Ingredients:

- 2 tsp olive oil
- 2 minced garlic cloves
- 1 shallot, minced
- 1,7lb (800 grams) of diced tinned tomatoes
- 1 cup broth made from vegetables 1 teaspoon dried oregano
- 0.5 grams dried oregano
- pepper and salt to flavor
- Basil fronds used as a garnish
- Whole wheat bread to be served

Preparation Guidelines:

1. Fry garlic and onion with oil for a few minutes.
2. Add the tinned tomatoes (including the juice), vegetable stock, dry basil, dried oregano, salt, and pepper to the saucepan. Mix well.
3. Lower heat and cook for about 15 or 20 minutes to allow tastes to meld.
4. Blend the soup until it is creamy.
5. Serve the Tomato Basil Soup steaming with fresh basil leaves as garnish. Complete and satiate your hunger with a slice of whole wheat bread.

Nutritional analysis per serving (soup only):

- Calories 120
- Fats 5g (0,7g Sat – 0 Trans)
- Cholesterol 0mg
- Sodium 700mg
- Carbs 16g
- Fibers 4g
- Sugars 9g
- Proteins 3g

Shopping List:

- Tomatoes
- Fresh basil
- Onion
- Garlic
- Low-sodium vegetable broth
- Whole wheat bread

Posible substitutions:

Use canned tomatoes if fresh are not available. Use low-sodium chicken stock instead of vegetable stock if preferred

Lentil and Spinach Soup with Turmeric

Lentil broth with Spinach and Turmeric is a nutritious and delicious broth that combines protein-rich lentils with vibrant spinach and the health benefits of turmeric. This substantial soup is rich in fiber, vitamins, and minerals, making it a scrumptious and nourishing option for lunch or dinner.

Ingredients:

- 1 shallot, minced
- 1 teaspoonful of olive oil
- 2 minced garlic cloves
- 0.5-milligram powdered cumin
- 4 cups vegetable stock 1 teaspoon turmeric powder
- 1 cup rinsed and drained green lentils, desiccated
- 2 cups of fresh spinach
- ½ teaspoon paprika
- pepper and salt to flavor

Preparation Guidelines:

1. Fry garlic and onion with oil for a few minutes.
2. Add lentils, vegetable stock, turmeric powder, cumin powder, paprika powder, salt, and pepper. Mix thoroughly to incorporate.
3. Cook for about 20 minutes on low-medium heat or until the lentils are tender.
4. Add the spinach and cook another 2 to 3 minutes.
5. Adjust the lentil soup's seasonings as necessary. For example, you may add salt, pepper, or herbs to taste.
6. Serve the soup, adding fresh lemon juice for added vivacity.
7. Complement the soup with whole grain bread or a salad to create a complete and satisfying entrée.

Nutritional analysis per serving (soup only):

- Calories: 250
- Fats 4g (0,5g Sat – 0g Trans)
- Cholesterol 0mg
- Sodium 800mg
- Carbs 41g
- Fibers 18g
- Sugars 4g
- Proteins 15g

Shopping List:

- Brown lentils
- Onion
- Carrots
- Celery
- Garlic
- Low-sodium vegetable broth
- Fresh spinach
- Turmeric

Possible substitutions:

Use other types of lentils, such as red or green. Use meat broth (preferably chicken) instead of vegetable broth. Use frozen spinach instead of fresh, if preferred.

Butternut Squash Soup with Coconut Milk

This recipe is a comforting and creamy soup that emphasizes the natural sweetness of butternut squash, which is enhanced by the richness of coconut milk. The flavor combination generates a velvety texture and a delightful equilibrium between sweetness and creaminess. This soup is ideal for comfortable evenings or a special occasion appetizer.

Ingredients:

- 1 medium-sized peeled, seeded, and diced butternut squash
- 2 chopped garlic cloves
- 1 shallot, minced 1 teaspoonful olive oil
- 1 tsp cinnamon powder
- ½ tsp powdered cinnamon
- 1 cup coconut milk
- 4 quarts vegetable stock
- pepper and salt to flavor
- For garnish, use fresh cilantro or parsley (optional).

Preparation Guidelines:

1. Spread the butternut squash cubes with oil on a baking sheet. To evenly coat the squash, toss it.
2. 30-35 minutes in an oven at 400°F/200°C or until the butternut squash is tender and faintly caramelized.
3. Sauteè some oil with garlic and onion
4. Add the roasted butternut squash cubes, cinnamon powder, and nutmeg powder to the broth. Stir well to incorporate, and allow the flavors to meld for several minutes.
5. Add the vegetables and cook until boiling. Simmer over low heat until the flavors are blended, and the soup has thickened, about 20 minutes.
6. Stir the broth until it is smooth and creamy.
7. Add the coconut milk. Avoid bringing the bouillon to a boil while warming it through.
8. Salt and pepper the Butternut Squash Soup with Coconut Milk to taste. Adjust seasoning as necessary.
9. If desirable, garnish with fresh coriander or parsley and ladle into bowls.
10. Warm the broth and serve it with crusty bread or a side salad for a delicious meal.

Nutritional analysis per serving (soup only):

- Calories: 220
- Fats 14g (10g Sat – 0g Trans)
- Cholesterol 0mg
- Sodium 450mg
- Carbs 24g
- Fibers 5g
- Sugars 5g
- Proteins 4g

Shopping List:

- Butternut squash
- Onion
- Garlic
- Low-sodium vegetable broth
- Coconut milk

Possible substitutions:

Use canned butternut squash if fresh is not available. Then replace the vegetable broth with the meat (preferably chicken). Almond milk instead of coconut milk.

Chicken and Vegetable Soup

Chicken and Vegetable broth is a hearty and nutritious broth made with tender chicken, a variety of colorful vegetables, and flavorful herbs. This soup is a complete supper in and of itself because it contains protein, vitamins, and minerals. It is ideal for warming you up on chilly days or under the weather.

Ingredients

- 2 minced celery stalks
- 2 minced garlic cloves
- 1 shallot, minced
- 2 carrots, minced
- 1 teaspoonful olive oil
- 1 minced red bell pepper
- 1 zucchini, sliced
- 4 cups of poultry stock
- 2 cups cooked, shredded or diced poultry
- 1 teaspoon rosemary leaves
- 1 bay leaf
- pepper and salt to flavor
- Fresh coriander used as garnish

Preparation Guidelines:

1. Fry garlic and onion with oil for a few minutes.
2. Add bell pepper, celery, carrots, and zucchini. For a few minutes, sauté the vegetables until they begin to soften.
3. Add the chicken broth, cooked chicken, bay leaf, dried thyme, salt, and pepper into a pan Mix thoroughly to incorporate.
4. Bring to a boil before then reduce to low heat. Cook until tender, about 20 minutes.
5. Add salt and pepper to adjust the soup's seasoning as necessary. Remove bay leaves before serving.
6. Garnish the Chicken and Vegetable Soup with fresh cilantro.
7. Serve hot with crusty bread for a nutritious and filling entrée.

Nutritional analysis per serving (soup only):

- Calories 220
- Fats 6g (1,5g Sat – 0g Trans)
- Cholesterol 45 mg
- Sodium 650mg
- Carbs 17g
- Fibers4g
- Sugars 7g
- Proteins 24g

Shopping List:

- Chicken breasts or thighs
- Carrots
- Celery
- Onion
- Garlic
- Low-sodium chicken broth

Possible substitutions:

Use frozen vegetables instead of fresh, if preferred

Minestrone Soup with Whole Wheat Pasta

Minestrone broth with Whole Wheat Pasta is a traditional Italian broth that is hearty, flavorful, and loaded with healthy ingredients. This vegetable-based soup's colorful vegetables, beans, and whole wheat pasta make it a filling and satisfying entrée.

Ingredients:

- 1 onion, sliced
- 1 teaspoonful olive oil
- cloves 2 carrots, minced
- 2 minced garlic
- 2 minced celery stalks
- 1 zucchini, sliced
- 1 cup of green beans, cleaned and cut into chunks
- 1 can (14 ounce) diced tomatoes
- 4 quarts vegetable stock
- 1 can (14 ounces) of drained and rinsed kidney beans
- 1 tsp powdered dry oregano
- ½ milligram of powdered thyme 1 tsp dried basil
- pepper and salt to flavor
- 1 cup whole wheat pasta (penne or fusilli, for example).
- Fresh coriander used as garnish
- Parmesan cheese grated for serving (optional)

Preparation Guidelines:

1. Sautee the oil, garlic, and onion
2. Add celery, carrots, zucchini, and green beans. For a few minutes, sauté the vegetables until they begin to soften.
3. Pour the diced tomatoes (including liquid) and vegetable broth into the pan. Mix thoroughly to incorporate.
4. Add the kidney beans that have been strained and rinsed, oregano, basil, thyme, salt, and pepper. Stir the ingredients again to incorporate them.
5. Bring to boil, then reduce to simmer. Cover the saucepan and cook for approximately 20 min. to allow the flavors to meld.
6. Cook the whole wheat pasta following the instructions on the package. Drain and reserve.
7. As soon as the broth has come to the boil, add the cooked whole grain pasta. Stir well and simmer for a further 5 minutes.
8. Adjust the soup's seasoning with salt and pepper as necessary.
9. Garnish the Minestrone Soup with Whole Wheat Pasta with fresh parsley.
10. Serve the broth hot, with grated Parmesan cheese for added richness if desired.

Nutritional analysis per serving (soup only):

- Calories: 250
- Fats 4g (0,5g Sat – 0 Trans)
- Cholesterol 0mg
- Sodium 750mg
- Carbs47g
- Fibers 10g
- Sugars 9g
- Proteins 10g

Shopping List:

- Low-sodium vegetable broth
- Onion
- Garlic
- Carrots
- Celery
- Canned tomatoes
- Kidney beans
- Whole wheat pasta

Possible substitutions:

Use chicken broth instead of vegetable broth. Use any canned beans instead of kidney beans. Use quinoa instead of pasta.

Black Bean Soup with Cilantro-Lime Cream

Black Bean broth with Cilantro-Lime Cream is a flavorful and satisfying broth that highlights black beans' earthy and robust flavors. This soup is seasoned with aromatic seasonings and topped with a zesty cilantro-lime cream. It is a great option for vegetarian or vegan meals and can be served as an appetizer or entrée.

Ingredients:

To prepare Black Bean Soup:

- 1 shallot, minced
- 2 tbsp olive oil
- 1 minced red bell pepper
- minced garlic cloves
- tablespoons cumin powder
- 1 tsp pepper powder
- 3 (15-ounce) cans of black beans, drained and rinsed
- ½ tsp smoked paprika
- 1 teaspoonful tomato paste
- 4 cups of vegetable stock
- Juice from one citrus
- Pepper and salt to flavor

For the Cilantro-Lime Cream, you should:

- 2 teaspoons fresh chopped cilantro
- 1/2 cup Greek yogurt or sour cream, plain
- Juice of half a citrus
- Salt to flavor

Preparation Guidelines:

1. Warm the oil in a large kettle over low-medium heat. Add the diced red bell pepper, minced onion, and minced garlic. Cook until the vegetables are fragrant.
2. Cumin, chili powder, and smoked paprika should be added to the saucepan. Stir well.
3. Combine the drained and rinsed black beans, vegetable broth, and tomato paste in a saucepan. Stir to incorporate.
4. Bring to a boil, then reduce to a simmer. Cover the saucepan and cook for approximately 20 min to allow the flavors to meld.
5. Prepare the cilantro-lime cream by combining the Greek yogurt or sour cream, chopped cilantro, lime juice, and salt in a small dish while the soup simmers. Stir until thoroughly combined. Set aside.
6. Blend the soup until smooth after the soup has boiled. This stage is optional, as some beans and vegetables can be left whole for texture.
7. Add lime juice, salt, and pepper.
8. Each portion of Black Bean Soup should be topped with a dollop of cilantro-lime cream.
9. If desired, serve the broth hot with additional cilantro and some lime juice.

Nutritional analysis per serving (soup only):

- Calories: 320
- Fats 8g (2g Sat – 0g Trans)
- Cholesterol 5 mg Sodium 720mg
- Carbs 47g
- Fibers 15g
- Sugars 4g
- Proteins 16g

Shopping List:

- Black beans
- Onion
- Garlic
- Low-sodium vegetable broth
- Cumin
- Lime
- Cilantro
- Greek yogurt

Possible substitutions:

Use canned black beans if dried are not available. Use chicken broth instead of vegetable broth.

Mushroom Barley Soup

Mushroom Barley Soup is a substantial and comforting soup that combines earthy mushrooms with nutritious barley. The combination of mushrooms, vegetables, and seasonings creates a savory and nourishing dish.

Ingredients:

- 1 onion, sliced
- 2 tsp olive oil
- 2 minced garlic cloves
- 8 oz diced white mushrooms
- 8 oz of cut cremini mushrooms
- 2 minced celery stalks
- 2 carrots, minced
- ½ cup pearl wheat
- 6 quarts vegetable stock
- 1 bay leaf
- 1 tsp rosemary leaves pepper and salt to flavor
- Fresh coriander used as garnish

Preparation Guidelines:

1. Fry the oil, garlic and onion.
2. Cremini mushrooms and white mushrooms should be added to the saucepan. Sauté the mushrooms until their moisture evaporates and they begin to caramelize.
3. Carrots, celery, and pearl barley should be added to the broth. To evenly coat the vegetables and barley with the savory mushroom mixture, incorporate well.
4. Pour the vegetable broth into the cauldron and add the bay leaf and dried thyme.
5. salt and pepper to taste
6. Bring to a boil, then reduce to a simmer. Cover the saucepan and cook for approximately 45-60 min or until tender.
7. While the Soup is simmering, chop fresh cilantro for the garnish.
8. Once the stock is complete, remove the bay leaf and discard it.
9. To serve, put some mushroom barley Soup into dishes and top with fresh parsley.
10. If desirable, accompany the Soup with crusty bread or a side salad.

Nutritional analysis per serving (soup only):

- Calories: 220
- Fats 8g (1g Sat – 0g Trans)
- Cholesterol 0mg
- Sodium 640mg
- Carbs 33g
- Fibers 6g
- Sugars 4g
- Proteins 6g

Shopping List:

- Onion
- Garlic
- Carrots
- Celery
- Low-sodium vegetable broth
- Mushrooms
- Barley

Possible ubstitutions:

Use chicken broth instead of vegetable broth. Use any type of mushrooms instead of white mushrooms, if preferred. Use quinoa instead of barley.

Carrot Ginger Soup with Greek Yogurt

Carrot Ginger broth with Greek Yogurt is a rich, flavorful broth that combines the sweetness of carrots and the heat of ginger. This broth is creamy, satiating, and nutrient-dense. Greek yogurt lends a tangy and creamy element that perfectly complements the other flavors.

Ingredients:

- 2 tsp olive oil
- 2 minced garlic cloves
- 1 shallot, chopped
- 1 pound of peeled and diced carrots
- 1 teaspoon minced ginger
- ½cup coconut milk
- 4 quarts vegetable stock
- 2 teaspoons fresh lime juice
- pepper and salt to flavor
- garnished with Greek yogurt and minced fresh cilantro

Preparation Guidelines:

1. Warm the olive oil in a large kettle over low-medium heat. Add the minced onion and garlic, and sauté until aromatic and softened.
2. Carrots and ginger are to be added to the stew. Mix thoroughly to incorporate.
3. Into the pot, pour the vegetable broth and boil. Reduce to low and cook the carrots for about 20 min. or until tender.
4. Remove from the heat. Leave to cool slightly.
5. Stir or blend the broth to make it creamy.
6. Reheat the kettle and stir in the lime juice and coconut milk. Add salt and pepper.
7. Warm the soup for a few minutes over moderate heat to thoroughly heat it.
8. Each serving of Carrot Ginger Soup should be garnished with a sprinkling of Greek yogurt and fresh cilantro.
9. If desirable, accompany the soup with crusty bread or a side salad.

Nutritional analysis per serving (soup only):

- Calories 180
- Fats 10g (4g Sat – 0g Trans)
- Cholesterol 0mg
- Sodium 580mg
- Carbs 20g
- Fibers 4g
- Sugars 8g
- Protein: 2g

Shopping List:

- Carrots
- Onion
- Garlic
- Ginger
- Low-sodium vegetable broth
- Greek yogurt

Possible substitutions:

Use chicken broth instead of vegetable broth. Use sour cream instead of Greek yogurt.

Quinoa Vegetable Soup

Quinoa Vegetable Soup is a healthy and nutritious soup with protein-rich quinoa and various vibrant vegetables. Combining quinoa, vegetables, and aromatic seasonings produces a comforting and flavorful dish.

Ingredients

- 2 teaspoons olive oil
- 1 shallot, minced
- 2 minced garlic cloves
- 2 carrots, minced
- 2 minced celery stalks
- 1 minced red bell pepper
- 1 zucchini, sliced
- 1 cup diced tomatoes
- ½ cup quinoa, rinsed
- 4 quarts vegetable stock
- 1 teaspoon rosemary leaves
- 1 teaspoon cumin powder
- pepper and salt to flavor
- Fresh coriander used as garnish

Preparation Guidelines:

1. Sautee the oil, garlic, and onion.
2. Celery, carrots, red bell pepper, and zucchini should be diced and added to the saucepan. For a few minutes, sauté the vegetables until they begin to soften.
3. Mix in the diced tomatoes, rinsed quinoa, vegetable broth, dried thyme, ground cumin, and salt and pepper.
4. Then bring to a boil and reduce to low the heat. Cover the saucepan and cook for approximately 15-20 min or until tender.
5. The Quinoa Vegetable Soup should be spooned into dishes and garnished with fresh parsley.
6. If desirable, accompany the soup with crusty bread or a side salad.

Nutritional analysis per serving (soup only):

- Calories 200
- Fats 6g (1g Sat – 0g Trans)
- Cholesterol 0mg
- Sodium 580mg
- Carbs 32g
- Fibers 7g
- Sugars 7g
- Proteins 6g

Shopping List:

- Quinoa
- Onion
- Garlic
- Carrots
- Celery
- Low-sodium vegetable broth

Possible substitutions:

Use chicken broth instead of vegetable broth. Use any type of vegetable instead of the listed ones.

Broccoli cheese soup with whole grain croutons

Broccoli Cheddar broth with Whole Grain Croutons is a comforting, cheesy broccoli-rich broth with whole grain croutons. The combination of creamy cheddar cheese and delicate broccoli results in a dish that is both flavorful and satisfying. Whole-grain croutons contribute a delectable crunch and texture.

Ingredients:

To make the Broccoli and Cheddar Soup:

- 2 teaspoons of butter
- 1 shallot, minced
- 2 minced garlic cloves
- 4 cups of vegetable stock
- 4 cups florets of minced broccoli
- 1 cup grated cheddar cheese
- 1 cup milk
- Pepper and salt to flavor

For the Whole Grain Croutons, you would:

- 2 tbsp cubes of whole grain bread
- 2 tbsp olive oil
- ½ milligram dried thyme
- ½ milligram dried oregano
- Pepper and salt to flavor

Preparation Guidelines:

1. Sautee butter, minced onion, and minced garlic in a large kettle
2. The broccoli florets should be added to the saucepan. Stir the broccoli to saturate it with the butter and onion mixture.
3. Boil the vegetable stock in a saucepan. Simmer over low heat for about 13-15 minutes or until tender.
4. Add the milk and cheddar cheese shreds. Stir the soup until the cheese has dissolved and it has become creamy.
5. Add salt and pepper to taste.
6. In a basin, combine the bread cubes, olive oil, dried thyme, dried oregano, salt, and pepper. To evenly coat the bread cubes, toss them.
7. Spread the bread cubes with the topping on a baking sheet. Bake in an oven at 385°F/195°C for about 10-15 minutes or until golden brown and crispy.
8. Allow the croutons to settle slightly after removing them from the oven.
9. Each bowl of Broccoli Cheddar Soup should be topped with a fistful of whole-grain croutons.
10. If desirable, garnish the soup with additional shredded cheddar cheese.

Nutritional analysis per serving (soup only):

- Calories: 300
- Fats 17g (8g Sat – 0g Trans)
- Cholesterol 35 mg
- Sodium 780mg
- Carbs 25g
- Fibers 5g
- Sugars 7g
- Proteins 13g

Shopping List:

- Broccoli
- Onion
- Garlic
- Low-sodium vegetable broth
- Cheddar cheese
- Whole grain bread

Possible substitutions:

Use chicken broth instead of vegetable broth. Use any cheese instead of cheddar. Use any bread instead of whole grain, if preferred.

SIDE DISH RECIPE

Balsamic Glazed Roasted Brussels Sprouts

Roasted Brussels Sprouts with Balsamic Glaze is a delectable and nutritious side dish highlighting Brussels sprouts' natural flavors. The roasting process amplifies their sweetness and imparts a crisp texture. In contrast, the balsamic glaze imparts a tart and faintly sweet note. This easy-to-prepare dish is the ideal accompaniment to any meal.

Ingredients:

- 2 teaspoons olive oil
- 1 pound Brussels sprouts, peeled and cut in half
- pepper and salt to flavor
- 2 teaspoons balsamic vinegar
- 1 teaspoon of honey (optional).
- Optional: 1 tablespoon of minced fresh parsley for garnish

Preparation Guidelines:

1. The Brussels sprouts should be evenly coated with oil, salt, and pepper.
2. On the prepared baking tray, place the Brussels sprouts in a single layer.
3. Roast in an oven at 400°F/200°C for approximately 30 minutes or until tender and golden, stirring midway through cooking to ensure even browning.
4. During the roasting of the Brussels sprouts, prepare the balsamic marinade. Combine the vinegar and honey (if using). Simmer the mixture for 3 or 5 minutes or until the glaze has thickened.
5. When the Brussels sprouts are cooked, remove them from the oven. Drizzle them with the balsamic marinade. Toss with care to saturate.
6. Transfer the roasted Brussels sprouts to a dish and, if desired, garnish with parsley.
7. As a nutritious side dish, immediately serve the roasted Brussels sprouts with balsamic marinade.

Nutritional analysis per serving:

- Calories: 150
- Fats 8g (1g Sat – 0g Tans)
- Cholesterol 0mg
- Sodium 40mg
- Carbs 18g
- Fibers 5g
- Sugars 8g
- Proteins 5g

Shopping List:

- Brussels sprouts
- Olive oil
- Salt and pepper
- Balsamic vinegar

Possible substitutions:

You can substitute the Brussels sprouts with other cruciferous vegetables like broccoli or cauliflower.

Quinoa Pilaf with Assorted Vegetables

Quinoa Pilaf with Mixed Vegetables is a nutritious and flavorful side dish that combines the earthy flavor of quinoa with an assortment of colorful vegetables. This pilaf is nutrient-dense and offers a delicious combination of textures and flavors. It is the ideal accompaniment to any main dish. However, it can also be savored as a light and satisfying meal.

Ingredients:

- 1 cup quinoa, rinsed
- 2 quarts vegetable stock
- 1 carrot, chopped
- 1 teaspoonful olive oil
- 1 zucchini, sliced
- 1 small onion, chopped
- 2 chopped garlic cloves
- 1 minced red bell pepper
- 1 cup frozen peas
- 1 tsp rosemary leaves
- pepper and salt to flavor
- Fresh parsley chopped for garnish (optional).

Preparation Guidelines:

1. Combine the vegetable and rinsed quinoa in a saucepan and boil over low-medium heat.
2. Cook covered for 15-20 minutes until all liquid is absorbed.
3. While the quinoa is simmering, warm the olive oil over medium heat in a skillet. Add the garlic and onion. Cook until the onion becomes translucent and aromatic.
4. Carrot, zucchini, and red bell pepper should be added to the skillet. Cook the vegetables for approximately 5 minutes or until they are barely tender.
5. Add the frozen peas and dried thyme and mix.
6. Cook until the peas are thoroughly heated (about 3 to 4 minutes.
7. Add to the vegetables when the quinoa is cooked.
8. Combine all ingredients until thoroughly combined.
9. Season the quinoa pilaf to flavor with salt and pepper. Adapt the seasoning as necessary.
10. Transfer the quinoa pilaf to a serving dish and, if desired, garnish with fresh cilantro.
11. Warm the quinoa pilaf with assorted vegetables and serve it as a nutritious and tasty side dish.

Nutritional analysis per serving:

- Calories 220
- Fats 6g (1g Sat – 0g Trans)
- Cholesterol 0mg
- Sodium 300mg
- Carbs 35g
- Fibers 6g
- Sugars 5g
- Protein 7g

Shopping List:

- Quinoa
- Mixed vegetables (such as carrots, peas, corn, and bell peppers)
- Garlic
- Olive oil
- Salt and pepper

Possible substitutions:

You can substitute the mixed vegetables with any seasonal vegetables you prefer, such as zucchini, eggplant, or mushrooms.

Asparagus Steamed with Lemon Zest

Steamed Asparagus with Lemon Zest is a simple, elegant side dish that accentuates asparagus' natural flavors. The crispness and vibrant green color of the asparagus are preserved by steaming. At the same time, adding lemon zest imparts a bright and refreshing citrus flavor. This dish is simple to prepare and complements a variety of entrees.

Ingredients:

- 1 pound of asparagus stalks with the tough ends trimmed off
- rind of one lemon
- 2 tbsp extra-virgin olive oil
- pepper and salt to flavor

Preparation Guidelines:

1. Place a steamer container inside a large pot containing a few inches of water.
2. Over low-moderate heat, bring the water to a boil.
3. Place the spears in the steamer in layers.
4. Cover the vessel and steam the asparagus until crisp-tender, approximately 4 to 6 minutes. Check for doneness by inserting a utensil into the thickest portion of an asparagus spear. Depending on how thick your spears are, the cooking time will vary. It should penetrate without much difficulty or resistance.
5. Once the asparagus has been steamed, transfer it gingerly to a serving platter.
6. Drizzle the oil over the steamed asparagus, taking care to uniformly coat each spear.
7. Distribute the lemon zest evenly over the asparagus spears.
8. Season the asparagus to flavor with salt and pepper.
9. Asparagus steamed with lemon zest, optionally served with lemon segments for additional acidity.

Nutritional analysis per serving:

- Calories 90
- Fats 7g (1g Sat – 0g Trans)
- Cholesterol 0mg
- Sodium 0mg
- Carbs 5g
- Fiber 3g
- Sugar 2g
- Protein 3g

Shopping List:

- Asparagus
- Lemon zest
- Olive oil
- Salt and pepper

Possible substitutions:

You can substitute the asparagus with other green vegetables like green beans or broccoli. For the lemon zest, you can use lime or orange zest instead.

Baked Sweet Potato Fries

This recipe is a delicious and nutritious alternative to traditional French fries. These fries are baked until perfectly crisp and seasoned with a blend of seasonings that accentuates their inherent sweetness. Everyone will appreciate them as a delightful side dish or tasty snack option.

Ingredients:

- 2 large peeled and sliced sweet potato fritters
- 2 tsp olive oil
- 1 tsp allspice
- ½ milligram of onion powder
- ½ milligram of garlic powder
- ½ milligram of powdered thyme
- pepper and salt to flavor
- Fresh parsley may be used as a garnish (optional).

Preparation Guidelines:

1. In a large basin, combine olive oil, onion powder, paprika, garlic powder, dry thyme, salt, and pepper with the sweet potato fries. Ensure that the potatoes are uniformly coated with seasoning.
2. Ensure the sweet potato fries are arranged in a single layer on the baking sheet.
3. To ensure even browning, bake the fries in an oven at 425°F/220°C for 20 to 25 minutes.
4. Turn off the oven when they are golden brown and firm.
5. Place the baked sweet potato fries on a serving platter and, if desired, garnish with cilantro.
6. The baked sweet potato fries are a delectable and nutritious side dish that should be served hot.

Nutritional analysis per serving:

- Calories: 150
- Fats 6g (1g Sat – 0g Trans)
- Cholesterol 0mg
- Sodium 150mg
- Carbs 24g
- Fibers 4g
- Sugars 5g
- Proteins 2g

Shopping List:

- Sweet potatoes
- Olive oil
- Paprika
- Salt and pepper

Possible substitutions:

You can substitute sweet potatoes with other root vegetables like carrots or parsnips. You can use cumin or chili powder instead of paprika for the seasoning.

Sautéed Spinach with Garlic

Garlic Sautéed Spinach is a nutritious and flavorful side dish that is quick and simple to prepare. Garlic is sautéed with spinach to impart a delectable aroma and flavor. It provides a wholesome dose of vitamins and minerals and is the ideal accompaniment to various main courses.

Ingredients:

- 1 pound of freshly rinsed and dried baby spinach leaves
- 2 chopped garlic cloves
- 1 teaspoonful olive oil
- pepper and salt to flavor
- Optional lemon wedges for presentation

Preparation Guidelines:

1. Start by heating some oil in a saucepan.
2. Add the garlic and cook for approximately one minute or until aromatic. Care must be taken not to roast the garlic.
3. Add the spinach in batches, allowing each load to wilt before adding more.
4. Turn and stir the spinach using tongs or a spatula to ensure even cooking.
5. About three to five minutes, or until wilted and tender, sauté the spinach.
6. Salt and pepper the spinach that has been sautéed to flavor.
7. Transfer the spinach cooked with garlic to a serving dish.
8. Serve the spinach hot, accompanied by lemon segments, for a tangy boost, if desired.

Nutritional analysis per serving:

- Calories 80
- Fats 4g (0g Sat – 0g Trans)
- Cholesterol 0mg
- Sodium 170mg
- Carbs 8g
- Fibers 4g
- Sugars 0g
- Proteins 5g

Shopping List:

- Spinach
- Garlic
- Olive oil
- Salt and pepper

Possible substitutions:

Other leafy vegetables, such as kale or Swiss chard, can be used instead of spinach. Substitute shallots or onions for garlic.

Brown Rice and Vegetable Medley

Brown Rice and Vegetable Medley is a healthy and satisfying side dish that combines the earthy flavors of brown rice with an assortment of colorful vegetables.

Ingredients:

- cup of raw brown rice
- quarts vegetable stock
- 1 teaspoonful olive oil
- 2 minced garlic cloves
- small onion, minced
- 1 small red bell pepper, sliced
- 1 cup halved cherry tomatoes
- 1 cup frozen kernels of maize
- 1 small zucchini, sliced
- 1 teaspoon rosemary leaves
- pepper and salt to flavor
- Fresh parsley may be used as a garnish (optional).

Preparation Guidelines:

1. Remove excess starch from the brown rice by rinsing it with cool water.
2. Combine rinsed brown rice and vegetable broth in a pot. Bring the liquid to a boil.
3. Cover the pot, and simmer for approximately 40-45 minutes.
4. Sauteè olive oil, minced garlic, and onion in a pan.
5. Red bell pepper and zucchini should be added to the pan. Continue cooking for an additional 4-5 minutes.
6. Stir in the maize kernels and cherry tomatoes from the freezer. Cook for about 2 minutes.
7. The vegetable mixture should be seasoned with dried thyme and salt and pepper to flavor. Mix thoroughly to incorporate.
8. Once the brown rice has been cooked, fluff it with a spatula and add it to the sautéed vegetables in the skillet. To distribute the ingredients equitably, gently toss the ingredients together.
9. Cook for another 3 to 4 minutes, allowing the flavors to combine.
10. The brown rice and vegetable mixture should be transferred to a serving dish.
11. If desirable, garnish with fresh parsley and serve as a nutritious and flavorful side dish.

Nutritional analysis per serving:

- Calories 220
- Fats 5g (0,5g Sat – 0g Trans
- Cholesterol 0mg
- Sodium 200mg
- Carbs 41g
- Fibers 5g
- Sugars 4g
- Proteins 5g

Shopping List:

- Brown rice
- Mixed vegetables (such as carrots, peas, corn, and bell peppers)
- Garlic
- Olive oil
- Salt and pepper

Possible substitutions:

You can substitute the mixed vegetables with any seasonal vegetables you prefer, such as zucchini, eggplant, or mushrooms.

Grilled Zucchini and Squashf

Grilled Zucchini and Squash is an easy and tasty side dish emphasizing these summer vegetables' natural flavors. Grilling them enhances their delicacy and imparts a subtle smokiness.

Ingredients:

- 2 midsize zucchini
- 2 yellow summer squash
- 2 teaspoons olive oil
- 1 teaspoon of powdered Italian spices
- pepper and salt to flavor
- Optional fresh basil stems for garnish

Preparation Guidelines:

1. Heat the grill over medium-high heat.
2. Cut the zucchini and pumpkin into rounds about 1/4-inch thick.
3. In a large bowl, mix the courgettes and pumpkin with olive oil, Italian seasoning, salt, and pepper. Ensure that the vegetables are uniformly coated.
4. Place the zucchini and squash segments on the grill grates that have been preheated—approximately four to five minutes per side.

Nutritional analysis per serving:

- Calories 80
- Fats 6g (1g Sat – 0g Trans)
- Cholesterol 0mg
- Sodium 5mg
- Carbs 7g
- Fibers 3g
- Sugars 4g
- Proteins 2g

Shopping List:

- Zucchini
- Squash
- Olive oil
- Salt and pepper

Possible substitutions:

You can substitute the zucchini and squash with other summer vegetables like eggplant or peppers. For the seasoning, you can use Italian seasoning or oregano instead.

Roasted Cauliflower with Turmeric

Roasted Cauliflower with Turmeric is a flavorful and nutritious side dish that highlights cauliflower's natural richness while adding a warm and earthy note from turmeric. The combination of roasting and seasonings produces a visually appealing and flavorful caramelized and aromatic cauliflower dish.

Ingredients:

- 1 large cauliflower head, minced into florets
- 1 teaspoon turmeric powder
- 2 teaspoons olive oil
- 0.5 milligram powdered cumin
- ½ tsp paprika
- ½ milligram of garlic powder
- pepper and salt to flavor
- Fresh parsley may be used as a garnish (optional).

Preparation Guidelines:

1. Combine the cauliflower florets, olive oil, turmeric powder, garlic powder, cumin powder, paprika, salt, and pepper.
2. Place the cauliflower florets on a greaseproof baking tray.
3. In the oven, roast the cauliflower for 25 to 30 minutes at 425°F/220°C or until golden brown and tender, stirring midway through to ensure even cooking.
4. After the cauliflowers have been roasted, could you put them in a serving dish?
5. Garnish with fresh parsley for a splash of color and added freshness.
6. As a flavorful and nutritious side dish, serve the turmeric-roasted cauliflower fresh.

Nutritional analysis per serving:

- Calories 120
- Fats 8g (1g Sat- 0g Trans)
- Cholesterol 0mg
- Sodium 80mg
- Carbs 10g
- Fibers 4g
- Sugars 4g
- Proteins 4g

Shopping List:

- Cauliflower
- Turmeric
- Olive oil
- Salt and pepper

Possible substitutions:

You can substitute the cauliflower with other cruciferous vegetables like broccoli or Brussels sprouts. For the seasoning, you can use cumin or coriander instead.

Green Beans Sautéed with Almonds

Sautéed Green Beans with Almonds is a straightforward and delicious side dish that adds a vibrant and wholesome component to any meal. The green beans are sautéed rapidly to preserve their crispness. The toasted almonds lend a delightful crunch and nutty flavor.

This dish is simple to prepare and pairs well with various entrees.

Ingredients:

- 1 pound fresh green beans, ends trimmed
- 2 teaspoons olive oil
- ¼ cup almonds cut
- 2 chopped garlic cloves
- pepper and salt to flavor
- Optional lemon wedges for presentation

Preparation Guidelines:

1. Saute the oil and garlic in a large pan.
2. Add the green beans and sauté for 5 to 7 minutes, or until they're vibrant green and crisp-tender. Occasionally stir the food to ensure even simmering.
3. While the green beans are simmering, place the sliced almonds in a small pan and heat them over low-medium heat. Toast them for approximately two to three minutes, stirring frequently, until aromatic and golden brown. Take precautions not to scorch them.
4. Once the green beans have reached the desirable tenderness, season them to taste with salt and pepper.
5. Serve the sautéed green beans with almonds steaming, accompanied by lemon wedges for a tangy kick if desired.

Nutritional analysis per serving:

- Calories 120
- Fats 9g (1g Sat – 0g Trans)
- Cholesterol 0mg
- Sodium 10mg
- Carbs 9g
- Fibers 4g
- Sugars 3g
- Proteins 3g

Shopping List:

- Green beans
- Garlic
- Olive oil
- Almonds
- Salt and pepper

Possible substitutions:

You can substitute the green beans with other vegetables like asparagus or broccoli. For the almonds, you can use other nuts like pine nuts or walnuts.

Quinoa and Black Bean

Quinoa and Black Bean Salad is a healthy and protein-rich side dish that is also satiating. Combining quinoa and black beans creates a complete plant-based protein source, while the vibrant vegetables and zesty dressing contribute freshness and flavor.

Ingredients:

- 1 cup prepared quinoa
- 1 cup halved cherry tomatoes
- 1 cup rinsed and strained black beans
- ½ cup diced cucumber
- ½ cup chopped red bell pepper
- ¼ teaspoon minced red scallion
- 2 teaspoons fresh chopped cilantro
- 1 ounce of lime
- 1 tsp cumin powder
- 2 tbsp extra-virgin olive oil
- pepper
- salt

Optional garnishes include avocado slices and feta cheese crumbles.

Preparation Guidelines:

1. Combine quinoa, black beans, red bell pepper, cherry tomatoes, cucumber, red onion, and cilantro.
2. Create the dressing by combining lime juice, olive oil, ground cumin, salt, and pepper.
3. Put the dressing over the mélange of quinoa and black beans.
4. Allow the salad to remain for at least 10 minutes so the flavors can combine.
5. If desirable, add avocado slices and crumbled feta cheese to the salad for added creaminess and acidity.
6. Serve the quinoa and black bean salad refrigerated or at room temperature and savor its nutrient-rich and flavorful qualities.

Nutritional analysis per serving:

- Calories 220
- Fats 10g (1,5g Sat – 0g Trans)
- Cholesterol 0mg
- Sodium 180mg
- Carbs 27g
- Fibers 8g
- Sugars 3g
- Proteins 8g

Shopping List:

- Quinoa
- Black beans
- Bell pepper
- Corn
- Red onion
- Cilantro
- Lime juice
- Olive oil
- Salt and pepper

Possible substitutions:

You can substitute the black beans with chickpeas or lentils. For the vegetables, you can use any seasonal vegetables you prefer, such as cucumber or tomato.

Oatmeal Applesauce Muffins

These Oatmeal Applesauce Muffins are a wholesome and satisfying delight ideal for breakfast or an on-the-go snack. These muffins are moist, flavorful, and have a delectable texture due to healthy ingredients such as oats and applesauce.

Ingredients:

- 1 ½ cups traditional oats
- 1 cup 100 percent whole wheat flour
- ¼ cup flaxseed meal
- 1 ounce of caramelized sugar
- 1 teaspoon baking powder
- ¾½ teaspoon baking soda
- ¼ tsp salt
- ½ tsp cinnamon powder
- 1 cup unadulterated unctuous apple sauce
- ¼ fluid ounce of honey or maple syrup
- ½ cup dairy or plant-based milk
- 1 tsp vanilla extract
- ½ cup almonds or dried fruits, chopped (optional)
- ¼ cup vegetable oil

Preparation Guidelines:

1. Make muffin pans out of paper and grease them with butter or paper or cooking spray (if you don't already have industrial muffin pans)
2. Mix the whole wheat flour, oats, flaxseed, brown sugar, baking powder, baking soda, cinnamon, and salt in a large basin.
3. Whisk together the applesauce, milk, honey or maple syrup, vegetable oil, and vanilla extract in a separate basin.
4. Put the liquid ingredients into the dry ingredients and stir until they are combined. Take caution not to overmix the ingredients.
5. Add chopped pecans or dried fruits to the muffin batter for added texture and flavor.
6. Into the prepared muffin cups, spoon the mixture (about 3/4 full).
7. Cook at 375°F/190°C for 15-20 minutes.
8. Remove from the oven and let them settle for a few minutes.
9. The oatmeal applesauce muffins may be served heated or at room temperature. Save leftovers for up to three days in a secure container at room temperature.

Nutritional analysis per serving (1 muffin):

- Calories 160
- Fats 6g (0,5g Sat – 0g Trans)
- Cholesterol 0mg
- Sodium 100mg
- Carbs 24g
- Fibers 3g
- Sugars 10g
- Proteins 3g

Shopping List:

- Rolled oats
- Eggs
- Cinnamon
- Baking soda
- Salt
- Baking powder
- Unsweetened applesauce
- Whole wheat flour
- Honey
- Milk
- Vanilla extract

Possible substitutions:

All-purpose flour can be used instead of wholemeal but is less nutritious. Maple syrup or agave nectar can replace honey. Almond milk or soymilk can be used instead of cow's milk.

APPETIZER RECIPES

Hummus with Fresh Vegetables from the Mediterranean

This Mediterranean Hummus with Fresh Vegetables is a delectable and wholesome appetizer that highlights the vibrant flavors of the Mediterranean. The combination of homemade hummus and an assortment of colorful fresh vegetables creates the ideal blend of textures and flavors. This appetizer is bound to impress your guests and satisfy your palate, whether you're hosting a party or simply craving a healthy snack.

Ingredients:

- ¼ cup tahini
- ¼ cup raw lemon juice
- 2 tps extra-virgin olive oil
- 2 minced cloves of garlic
- 2 tsp sal
- 0.5 milligram powdered cumin
- 2 (15-ounce) cans of drained and rinsed legumes
- to flavor, freshly ground black pepper
- Servings of assorted fresh vegetables (including bell peppers, cucumber, carrots, and cherry tomatoes, etc.).

Preparation Guidelines:

1. Combine the chickpeas, lemon juice, tahini, minced garlic, oil, ground cumin, salt, and black pepper in a food processor until it is creamy. If the hummus is too thick, additional olive oil or water can be added to obtain the desired consistency.
2. Put the hummus in a basin and garnish with olive oil, cumin, and fresh herbs, if desired.
3. Wash, peel, and cut into bite-sized portions of the fresh vegetables.
4. Arrange the raw vegetables on a platter or serving tray around the hummus bowl.
5. Serve the hummus alongside the raw vegetables for dipping.

Nutritional analysis per serving (2 tbsp hummus with vegetables):

- Calories 120
- Fats 6g (0,5g Sat – 0g Trans)
- Cholesterol 0mg
- Sodium 160mg
- Carbs 13g
- Fibers 4g
- Sugars 2g
- Proteins 4g

Shopping List:

- Chickpeas
- Tahini
- Garlic
- Lemon juice
- Olive oil
- Salt
- Fresh vegetables such as carrots, celery, bell peppers, and cucumbers

Possible substitutions:

For a lower-fat option, use less olive oil and more water in the hummus recipe. Use a variety of vegetables based on personal preference and availability.

Baked Spinach and Artichoke Dip

This Baked Spinach and Artichoke Dip is a timeless appetizer that never fails to delight a large group. This dip combines spinach, artichoke hearts, and a mixture of cheeses for a creamy and flavorful indulgence. The warm, gooey texture created by baking it to golden perfection combines well with tortilla chips or toasted bread. This dip will be a hit whether you are hosting a party or simply searching for a tasty snack.

Ingredients:

- 1 cup minced mozzarella cheese
- 1 can of artichoke hearts (14 ounces), drained and sliced
- 1 package (10 ounces) of thawed and pressed frozen spinach
- ½ cup of minced Parmesan
- ½ teaspoon dried rosemary
- ½ cup sour cream
- 2 minced cloves of garlic
- ½ cup mayonnaise
- 0.5 grams dried oregano
- ¼ milligram of black pepper
- ¼ tsp salt

Preparation Guidelines:

1. Combine spinach, chopped artichoke hearts, mozzarella cheese, Parmesan cheese, mayonnaise, sour cream, minced garlic, dried basil, dry oregano, salt, and black pepper in a mixing basin.
2. Transfer the mixture to an even layer in a casserole dish or cast-iron skillet.
3. Bake for approximately 18 to 20 minutes at 350°F/175°C in a preheated oven.
4. Before serving, allow to chill for a few minutes.
5. Serve the baked spinach and artichoke sauce with tortilla chips, toasted bread, or other dipping accompaniments of your choosing.

Nutritional analysis per serving (2 tablespoons):

- Calories 120
- Fats 9g (3g Sat – 0g Trans)
- Cholesterol 15mg
- Sodium 280mg
- Carbs 5g
- Fibers 1g
- Sugars 1g
- Proteins 4g

Shopping List:

- Sour cream
- Canned artichoke hearts
- Cream cheese
- Frozen spinach
- Garlic powder
- Parmesan cheese
- Mayonnaise
- Black pepper
- Salt

Possible substitutions:

For a lower-fat option, use Greek yogurt instead of sour cream. Use reduced-fat cream cheese and mayonnaise for a healthier option. Use fresh spinach instead of frozen if available.

Caprese Skewers with Balsamic Glaze

These Caprese Skewers with Balsamic Glaze are a delectable appetizer that combines the flavors of fresh tomatoes, mozzarella cheese, and basil exquisitely. These bite-sized delights, which are skewered and drizzled with a tart balsamic glaze, are both visually appealing and bursting with Mediterranean flavors. These easy-to-assemble skewers are ideal for any occasion. They will impress your visitors with their vibrant colors and delicious flavor.

Ingredients:

- ripe tomatoes
- Fresh mozzarella spheres
- Basil fronds grown from the ground
- Balsamic glazing
- pepper and salt to flavor
- Skewers (wooden or metal)

Preparation Guidelines:

1. Wash and dry cherry tomatoes with a kitchen roll. The mozzarella balls have been cut into bite-sized portions.
2. To construct each skewer, thread a cherry tomato, a piece of mozzarella, and a fresh basil leaf onto a skewer. Repeat the procedure until each skewer is filled.
3. Arrange the skewers on a plate for serving.
4. Pour the balsamic glaze into the skewers and evenly saturate each skewer.
5. Add salt and pepper.
6. Immediately serve the Caprese skewers so your guests can appreciate the vibrant flavors and textures.

Nutritional analysis per serving (2 skewers):

- Calories 80
- Fats 5g (3g Sat – 0g Trans)
- Cholesterol 15mg
- Sodium 80mg
- Carbs 4g
- Fibers 0g
- Sugars 3g
- Proteins 5g

Shopping List:

- Cherry tomatoes
- Fresh basil leaves
- Mozzarella cheese
- Balsamic vinegar
- Olive oil
- Salt
- Black pepper

Possible substitutions:

Use grape tomatoes instead of cherry tomatoes. Use reduced-fat mozzarella cheese for a lower-fat option. Use a calorie-reduced balsamic icing or make it yourself using balsamic vinegar reduced in a pan.

Mushrooms Stuffed with Quinoa and Feta

These Stuffed Mushrooms with Quinoa and Feta are a delicious appetizer that is certain to impress your guests. These bite-sized treats are filled with texture and flavor thanks to a combination of earthy mushrooms, savory quinoa, and creamy feta cheese. The mushrooms are stuffed with a delectable mixture of cooked quinoa, feta cheese, herbs, and seasonings, resulting in a tasty and wholesome appetizer.

Ingredients:

- 12 substantial button mushrooms
- 1 minced garlic shallot
- ¼ cup of shredded feta
- 2 tbsp red onion finely minced
- 0.5 grams dried oregano
- ¼ cup prepared quinoa
- 2 tbsp of fresh parsley, finely minced
- pepper and salt to flavor
- Olive oil to be used for scrubbing

Preparation Guidelines:

1. Place the baking tray on greaseproof paper.
2. Remove the mushrooms from the stems to make room for stuffing. Cut the branches of the mushrooms into small pieces and set aside.
3. Combine the cooked quinoa, crumbled feta cheese, chopped mushroom stems, red onion, parsley, dried oregano, minced garlic, and salt and pepper in a mixing basin. Mix thoroughly to incorporate all ingredients.
4. Coat the mushroom crowns with olive oil, then arrange them on the baking sheet.
5. Fill each mushroom cap with a teaspoon of the quinoa and feta mixture, delicately pressing it into the cavity.
6. Bake the loaded mushrooms for 15 to 20 min in an oven at 375°F/190°C.
7. Serve the stuffed mushrooms as an appetizer or party snack and revel in their delectable flavor combination.

Nutritional analysis for two mushrooms per serving:

- Calories 90
- Fats 5g (1,5g Sat – 0g Trans)
- Cholesterol 5mg
- Sodium 150mg
- Carbs 11g
- Fibers 2g
- Sugars 1g
- Proteins 4g

Shopping List:

- Mushrooms
- Red onion
- Feta cheese
- Quinoa
- Garlic
- Salt
- Black pepper
- Olive oil

Possible substitutions:

Use low-fat cottage cheese or ricotta instead of feta for a lower-fat option. Use other vegetables, such as bell peppers or zucchini, instead of the red onion. Add spinach or kale to the quinoa stuffing for added nutrition.

Cucumber and Greek yogurt dip with pita chips made from whole wheat.

This refreshing Cucumber and Greek Yogurt Dip is a healthy appetizer that combines perfectly with pita chips made from whole wheat. The combination of cold cucumber, tart Greek yogurt, and aromatic herbs results in a creamy and flavorful dip that is ideal for entertaining or snacking. The dip is simple to prepare and pairs well with homemade whole-wheat pita crackers for a satisfying crunch.

Ingredients:

For the bottom

- 1 minced garlic shallot
- 1 tiny cucumber, seeded and diced coarsely
- 1 pint of Greek yogurt
- 2 tablespoons minced fresh dill
- pepper
- 1 teaspoonful fresh lemon juice
- salt

To prepare pita chips:

- 4 whole grain pitas
- Olive oil to be used for scrubbing
- pepper and salt to flavor

Preparation Guidelines:

1. Mix the Greek yogurt, cucumber, garlic, lemon juice, and fresh dill in a basin. Mix thoroughly to combine all ingredients.
2. Salt and pepper to season. Adapt the seasoning to your taste preferences.
3. To allow the flavors to meld, cover the dip and put it in the fridge for at least 30 minutes.
4. Cut the pitas made with whole wheat into triangle-shaped wedges.
5. Brush both sides of the pita wedges with a drizzle of olive oil before placing them on a baking tray.
6. Bake the pita pieces in an oven at 375°F/190°C for approximately 10 to 12 min.
7. Allow the pita chips to cool thoroughly after removing them from the oven.
8. Serve the cucumber and Greek yogurt dip alongside the pita crackers made from whole wheat flour.
9. This delectable appetizer features energizing tastes and a satisfying crunch.

Nutritional analysis per portion (two tablespoons of dip and eight pita chips):

- Calories 120
- Fats 3g (0,5g Sat – 0g Trans)
- Cholesterol 0mg
- Sodium 180mg
- Carbs 19g
- Fibers 3g
- Sugars 2g
- Proteins 6g

Shopping List:

- Greek yogurt
- Cucumber
- Lemon juice
- Garlic
- Fresh dill
- Salt
- Whole wheat pita bread

Possible substitutions:

Use reduced-fat or non-fat Greek yogurt for a lower-fat option. Use parsley or basil instead. Use different vegetables carrots or bell peppers) for dipping.

30-Days Meal Plan Recipes

This contains an assortment of heart-healthy recipes that are simple and delectable. These recipes are easy to prepare and full of heart-healthy nutrients, whether you're a novice or an experienced chef. This chapter contains breakfast, lunch, and dinner recipes, so it has something for everyone.

	BREAKFAST	DINNER	LUNCH
1	Egg Muffins with Spinach and Mushrooms	Grilled Lemon and Herb Chicken with Quinoa Salad	Tomato Basil Soup with Whole Wheat Bread
2	Whole Wheat Pancakes with Fresh Berries	Salmon with Roasted Vegetables	Lentil and Spinach Soup with Turmeric
3	Greek Yogurt Parfait and Fruits	Vegetable and Lentil Stir-Fry	Butternut Squash Soup with Coconut milk
4	Oatmeal with Chia and Almonds	Turkey and Vegetable Lettuce Wraps	Chicken and Vegetables Soup
5	Avocado Toast with Poached Egg	Quinoa Stuffed Bell Peppers	Minestrone Soup with Whole Wheat Pasta
6	Veggie Breakfast Burritos	Recipe for Squash Spaghetti with Tomato Basoil Sauce	Black Bean Soup with Cilantro-Lime Cream
7	Quinoa Breakfast Bowl with ixed Berries	Brown Rice Grilled Shrimp Skeers	Mushroom Barley Soup
8	Egg Muffins with Spinach and Mushrooms	Cod Baked with a Lemon-dill Sauce	Carrot Ginger Soup with Greek Yogurt
9	Blueberry Almond Smoothie Bowl	Chickpea and Vegetable Curry	Quinoa Vegetable soup
10	Sweet Potato Hash with Turkey Sausage	Portobello Mushrooms Burgers Grilled	Brocoli Cheese Soup with Whole Grain

	BREAKFAST	DINNER	LUNCH
11	Egg Muffins with Spinach and Mushrooms	Tomato Basil Soup with Whole Wheat Bread	Grilled Lemon and Herb Chicken with Quinoa Salad
12	Whole Wheat Pancakes with Fresh Berries	Lentil and Spinach Soup with Turmeric	Salmon with Roasted Vegetables
13	Greek Yogurt Parfait and Fruits	Butternut Squash Soup with Coconut milk	Vegetable and Lentil Stir-Fry
14	Oatmeal with Chia and Almonds	Chicken and Vegetables Soup	Turkey and Vegetable Lettuce Wraps
15	Avocado Toast with Poached Egg	Minestrone Soup with Whole Wheat Pasta	Quinoa Stuffed Bell Peppers
16	Veggie Breakfast Burritos	Mushroom Barley Soup	Recipe for Squash Spaghetti with Tomato Basoil Sauce
17	Quinoa Breakfast Bowl with ixed Berries	Carrot Ginger Soup with Greek Yogurt	Brown Rice Grilled Shrimp Skeers
18	Egg Muffins with Spinach and Mushrooms	Quinoa Vegetable soup	Cod Baked with a Lemon-dill Sauce
19	Blueberry Almond Smoothie Bowl	Brocoli Cheese Soup with Whole Grain	Portobello Mushrooms Burgers Grilled
20	Sweet Potato Hash with Turkey Sausage	Chicken and Vegetables Soup	Chickpea and Vegetable Curry

	BREAKFAST	DINNER	LUNCH
21	Egg Muffins with Spinach and Mushrooms	Tomato Basil Soup with Whole Wheat Bread	Grilled Lemon and Herb Chicken with Quinoa Salad
22	Whole Wheat Pancakes with Fresh Berries	Salmon with Roasted Vegetables	Lentil and Spinach Soup with Turmeric
23	Greek Yogurt Parfait and Fruits	Butternut Squash Soup with Coconut milk	Vegetable and Lentil Stir-Fry
24	Oatmeal with Chia and Almonds	Turkey and Vegetable Lettuce Wraps	Chicken and Vegetables Soup
25	Avocado Toast with Poached Egg	Minestrone Soup with Whole Wheat Pasta	Quinoa Stuffed Bell Peppers
26	Veggie Breakfast Burritos	Recipe for Squash Spaghetti with Tomato Basoil Sauce	Mushroom Barley Soup
27	Quinoa Breakfast Bowl with ixed Berries	Carrot Ginger Soup with Greek Yogurt	Brown Rice Grilled Shrimp Skeers
28	Egg Muffins with Spinach and Mushrooms	Cod Baked with a Lemon-dill Sauce	Quinoa Vegetable soup
29	Blueberry Almond Smoothie Bowl	Brocoli Cheese Soup with Whole Grain	Portobello Mushrooms Burgers Grilled
30	Sweet Potato Hash with Turkey Sausage	Chickpea and Vegetable Curry	Chicken and Vegetables Soup

CONCLUSION

Those looking to begin a heart-healthy diet find the "Heart-Healthy Cookbook for Beginners 2023" a fantastic resource. The cookbook contains delicious meals that are also heart disease-preventing due to their low levels of sodium, saturated and trans fats, added sugars, and other unhealthy ingredients.

The cookbook strongly emphasizes the value of including whole grains, lean protein, heart-healthy fats, fruits, and vegetables in one's diet. To maintain optimal heart health, it lists the foods and substances that should be avoided or consumed in moderation, including salt, bread and baked goods, sugary drinks, and alcoholic beverages.

Additionally, the cookbook offers alternatives and modifications for every recipe, giving readers the freedom to alter their meals to suit their dietary requirements and preferences. The cookbook is perfect for novices new to healthy eating or anyone who wants to enhance their heart health because it includes clear directions and practical tips.

Overall, those who wish to take control of their health and make positive dietary changes will find the "Heart Healthy Cookbook for Beginners 2023" a helpful resource. Readers can enjoy tasty meals while lowering their risk of heart disease and enhancing their general well-being by implementing the recipes and instructions in the cookbook.

Printed in Great Britain
by Amazon

25029167R00053